man·i·fes·to (n) : a public declaration of

motives and intent

The SEO Manifesto™

A PRACTICAL AND ETHICAL GUIDE TO
EFFECTIVE INTERNET MARKETING AND
SEARCH ENGINE OPTIMIZATION (SEO)

Pam Gobiel

Dan Tousignant

Printed in the United States of America

First Printing, 2011

ISBN 978-0-9848767-0-9

Published by:

Cape Project Management, Inc.
12 Remington Lane
Plymouth, MA 02360
508-728-3614

Visit us at http://www.SeoManifesto.com

Table of Contents

Chapter 1: Getting Started

The SEO Manifesto

"It is my intent that, through my actions and by my willingness to learn, I will create a successful online business.

I will ethically attract customers to my website, where I will offer products, services, or information that have value.

By virtue of this intention, I will gain the freedom to work from home or anywhere in the world."

The above statement is the manifesto by which we choose to live and grow our business. It expresses the intent with which this guide was written. We hope you join us in making this your manifesto as you embark on the exciting challenge of launching your internet business.

– the authors, Dan Tousignant and Pam Gobiel

Who should read this Guide?

- Do you have a small business that you want to promote on the internet?

- Do you have an existing internet business? Do you want to increase traffic to your website?

- Are you interested in starting a new online business and do not know where to start?

If you answered "yes" to any of these questions, this guide is for you. Whether you are a web site designer, small business owner, or an entrepreneur looking to understand internet marketing and search engine optimization, we will ensure that reading this guide is worth your time and effort.

The purpose of this guide is to introduce you to the methods, processes, and tools to increase the traffic to your website. This guide is a practical guide, not only for learning the critical information you need, but to also walk you through, in a step-by-step approach, launching, maintaining, and improving your online business. It is intended to guide you through each phase of launching an online business, from how to get it off the ground to how to successfully maintain it.

Using this guide

This guide is designed as a resource for **you**, the person who is putting in the time and effort growing an online business. It is divided into the following chapters which reflect the phases you will go through as you build and grow your internet business:

Prepare: explains how to develop an internet marketing plan

Launch: walks you through how to get your website launched

Optimize: explains how to design or modify your site to be optimized for search engines

Submit: describes how to take advantage of different tools to ensure your visibility on the internet

Network: teaches you how to attract customers through social and business networking

Advertise: addresses the free and paid options for advertising your online business

Track: defines and prioritizes the information you need in order to monitor and manage your online business

Maintain: identifies the processes and tools needed to maintain and grow your internet presence

Each chapter includes a checklist, process description, and examples. If you have not launched your business yet, then work through the checklist in each chapter, starting with the first one. If your business is underway, you should begin by reviewing the first few chapters until you reach the section of the book that you have not yet implemented for your business.

Once you complete a phase and complete the checklist, you should move to the next phase. This guide is intended to be followed in a sequential fashion, but it is not mandatory. Continue with this approach until you have completed all of the checklists. You can use this guide to document your progress, or you can use the standalone checklist in the Appendix*.

*If you purchased this as an eBook, or if you would like an electronic version of the checklist, (go to www.SeoManifesto.com/appendix/ to download the checklist and get online access to the rest of the Appendix resources.

Pronouns

For the most part, we speak in first-person singular rather than first-person plural in the rest of this book. (We say "I," not "we.") We include a lot of personal anecdotes and experiences, and the singular form works better as a result. However, this book is unquestionably the result of a partnership between two authors and our use of the word "I" is merely a convenience. We use this style to ensure that you are clear that everything we review in this book is a result of our personal experiences and our trial and error approach. We are not academics spouting theoretical approaches. We are practical, hands-on entrepreneurs who are walking you through, in detail, how we have been successful and hoping that you can be too.

What is...?

This section answers some commonly-asked questions about terminology related to internet marketing and SEO. We will refer to these terms throughout this guide and expand on their definitions.

What is SEO?

SEO or search engine optimization simply refers to improving where you show up on an internet search. Search engines crawl your site looking for terms or keywords which tell them what your site is about. Essentially, the more the search engines understand your site, the higher your site will show up on related results.

SEO has also become a more generic term used in the industry to encompass all of the different internet marketing techniques that can be applied to your site to optimize your relationship with the search engine. Actual SEO can be addressed in several different ways:

- Site Content: How much content is on your site and how does it all relate?

- Site Design: Does the design of your site help or hurt the ability for search engines to find you?

- Internet Presence: How is your site recognized on the internet by other sites?

SEO techniques are constantly changing. Once it was as simple as having the appropriate keywords in your *meta data* or hidden fields on your web pages. Now, Google does not even look at these hidden keywords because of the increase in keyword spamming.

Why is SEO important to you?

The goal of search engine optimization, or SEO, is to get you to show up high in search results if someone is searching on a term related to your website. If you do not show up on the first three pages of search results, potential customers are less likely to find you. SEO encompasses all the strategies used to bring more traffic to your site "organically." By organically, we refer to the industry term that describes how to attract customers to your site without paying for advertising. This guide is dedicated to primarily growing your business organically by applying processes, investing time, putting forth effort, and having patience.

The opposite of organic growth is paid advertising. The advantage of organic growth is it is essentially "free," but free does not mean easily or quickly. Traditional advertising and marketing drives the bulk of traffic to many of the most prosperous sites on the internet. GoDaddy.com's Superbowl ads have driven much more traffic to their site than a typical organic SEO strategy would have.

That is not to say that we do not recommend paid advertising. We do. We will address paid advertising in this guide. A paid advertising strategy should complement your organic growth strategy.

Paid advertising is especially critical if you are looking to increase traffic in the short term. Traditional advertising such as newspaper, radio, television, and billboards can all drive traffic to your site. We will not address those approaches in this book. Rather, we will address the use of online providers and the pay per click (PPC) approach to increase traffic to your website.

Who are the authors?

Dan Tousignant is a habitual entrepreneur who has launched several businesses including project management consulting and training, and more recently, online affiliate businesses. Both as an employee and consultant, Dan has over 20 years of business management experience. He has managed software and web development projects for several Fortune® 500 companies with annual project budgets of over 10 million dollars. His experience in SEO and internet marketing began in 1996 when Dan took his first HTML class and developed his first commercial website.

One of the most effective services that Dan has offered over the years is the development and delivery of project management processes and tools. Dan's role has been to simplify the complex processes used to manage large projects into step-by-step procedures in order to train project managers and to increase the opportunity for project success. As you will see, it is just this skill that Dan has brought to the creation of this guide.

Pam Gobiel was introduced to internet marketing through a completely different path. Until 2002, Pam was a senior executive assistant for one of the largest investment firms in the country. Due to health reasons, she became homebound. Given her inclination as a high performer and her desire to be part of a professional community, Pam began designing and developing products for one of the most successful online drop-ship vendors. Doing this allowed her to run an international business, without having to leave her home or computer.

Pam has always been comfortable with computers and learning new tools. As a web-based entrepreneur, she exploited those skills and became an expert in internet marketing and SEO. In the past five years, Pam has evolved from having a fun online hobby to having a six-figure income. As a result, her husband made the decision to close his construction company and work with her from home. It has also given them the freedom to buy an RV to travel, visit friends, and meet Pam's online acquaintances with whom she has built relationships over the years.

Why the SEO Manifesto?

Dan has been friends with Pam's husband, Marc, for years, and they often have dinners together. At one of the dinners, while Pam and Dan were discussing their current careers, there was one of those transcendental moments that only happen a few times in life. Pam and Dan realized that a wonderful opportunity to work together was staring them right in the face.

Pam mentioned how her business had grown so much that she needed to hire people to perform certain steps to maintain her SEO. Unfortunately, she had never really documented everything she does, so it was continuously a challenge hiring and training people. Not only that, but people were always asking her what she does to be so successful. She began to realize there was no easy answer, because it was something that was complex, and it required time and patience.

Dan mentioned how he loved where he was in his career because he was developing and delivering training that was continuously receiving positive reviews. It was due, in most part, to his ability to tie in theoretical learning with his real life experience and a practical approach.

That is when the SEO Manifesto was born. We began talking right then about creating a SEO training using Pam's knowledge and Dan's training expertise. The discussion gave birth to the SEO

Training Group, www.SEOTraniningGroup.com. Soon after, when we realized we could only reach a small audience with classroom training, we decided to create The SEO Manifesto.

The SEO Manifesto is the serendipitous result of collaboration between Dan and Pam. It reflects our combined commitment to running our businesses, and it was the impetus to naming this guide. It is the culmination of knowledge and experience from experts in SEO and process development. What started as a curriculum for a training course has evolved into a step-by-step approach to launching and building a business on the internet.

So, we invite you to read, apply, and enjoy your path down a road, which is paved with our experience, trials and errors, lessons learned, and proven successes.

What do we mean by ethical?

You will notice that this guide is described as "practical and ethical." We specifically wanted to create a guide that was unique. We wanted it to be a practical approach, and one that did not promote the many unethical practices that have been adopted by people who are trying to increase their SEO. We sought to focus on only those practices that are ethical. The industry has coined the term "black hat" internet marketing for those strategies that have questionable ethical approaches. Examples of these are:

- White Text: one of the first ways that developers used to trick search engines. They put hundreds of keywords on the home page hidden in the same color as the background, usually white.

- False Redirects: creating a page that is high-ranked on the search engine but is never seen by the visitor and which you are redirected to another page automatically.

- Spamming Forums and Comments: creating posts to blogs and forums that are erroneous but include your webpage link.

Though these types of approaches may increase your traffic in the short term, they will only hurt you in the long term. As new "black hat" approaches are developed, search engines are modified to ignore these techniques. In many cases, they can get you banned by the search engine provider. In addition, when potential customers realize that they have been tricked, they will not be loyal to your business. All of the techniques and approaches discussed in this book have an ethical intent. That is not to say that someone cannot find a way to exploit these techniques unethically, but we can only be responsible for the intent our message, not the wayward application.

How quickly will I see the results?

If you follow the steps in this guide, you will see some results immediately. Significant organic results take time, effort, and patience. If you perform the steps in each of the phases in this guide, you should see the results listed below:

Launch Phase:
- Your website with your domain name will show up within 1 hour to 3 days.

- Search engines will index your site within 1 to 4 weeks (depending on the search engine).

Optimization Phase:
- If you only perform this phase, you will show up in organic keyword search results within 3-6 months.

Submission Phase:
- Once you have completed this phase, you may have improved keyword search results within 1-3 months.

Networking Phase:

- This phase could have an immediate impact to your website traffic.

Advertising Phase:

- This phase will have an immediate impact to your website visibility and traffic.

Maintenance Phase

- This ongoing phase should show gradual improvement every month.

On which Search Engine should I focus?

At the time of this printing, www.comScore.com listed the following market share for search engines[i]:

Search Entity	April 2011
Google Sites	65.4%
Yahoo! Sites	15.9%
Microsoft Sites	14.1%
Ask Network	3.0%
AOL, Inc.	1.5%

Given these results, most of our examples focus on Google®, but our approach is still applicable to Yahoo!®, Bing®, and others. If your site is optimized for Google, it will most likely be optimized for the other search engines as well, though there are differences in their search algorithms. Algorithms are the rules that search engines use to rank your site in their results. This guide does not get into detail about the computations and math behind these algorithms, as they are too complex and constantly changing.

In many ways those algorithms are not much different from Coke's® secret recipe. They do not want you to know every component because competitors will be able to copy them, and you will be able to rig your website for the search engine and not for the visitor.

If you are interested in understanding more about these algorithms, or you are just curious, enter "search engine algorithms" into any search engine and you will have a storehouse of good (and technical) information.

What do these terms mean?

Below you will find many of the common terms and acronyms frequently seen both in this book and throughout the web in regard to SEO. This list is not all-inclusive. We have also put this glossary in the Appendix as a quick reference.

301	Status Code: tells search engines if you have moved or deleted a web page
404	Status Code: Not Found – the result you see if you go to a web page that no longer exists
Abandonment Rate	The rate at which begin the process of performing your Call to Action but never complete it.
Affiliate	Someone who has a license agreement to market another company's goods or services usually for a commission based upon a sale, a click or a lead
B2B	Business to Business

B2C	Business to Consumer
BODY	The portion of an HTML document that contains the document's content
Bounce Rate	The percentage of people who exit the site after only viewing one page
Call to Action	A response that you want to get from a visitor on your site including a purchase, survey or download.
CPC	Cost Per Click: the typical way online advertisers charge. You pay only if someone clicks on your ad
CPM	CPM or Cost per thousand (the M represent the roman numeral for 1000)
Crawl	A slang term used to define how search engines find your site and all of its associated pages
CTR	Click Through Rate: the percentage of people who click on your website link out of the total number who see it
DMOZ	Directory Mozilla: the largest free online directory of websites
DNS	Domain Name System
FAQ	Frequently Asked Question
FTP	File Transfer Protocol
H1, H2, H3, H4, H5, H6	Heading Levels 1, 2, 3, 4, 5, 6: A heading format element in HTML

HEAD	The HEAD element is the portion of HTML document that contains hidden information about a web page, such as its title and keywords
HTML	Hypertext Markup Language: the primary language in which web pages are written
Impressions	The number of times a webpage or advertisement is shown to a visitor
Index	Where search engines collect and store information about a website
ISP	Internet Service Provider
META	Metadata: the hidden information in the HEAD of HTML that defines certain aspects about your website for search engines <meta http-equiv="content-type" content=""> <meta name="robots" content=""> <meta name="description" content=""> <meta name="keywords" content=""> <meta name="author" content="">
SEM	Search Engine Marketing
SEO	Search Engine Optimization
SERPs	Search Engine Results Pages
TITLE	Document Title: in the HEAD of HTML where authors should identify the contents of a web page

Troll	A person who comments on public forums to either sabotage the blog or promote unrelated products or services
URL	Uniform Resource Locator: http://www.example.com
W3C	World Wide Web Consortium
XML	Extensible Markup Language (file.xml)

Chapter 2: Prepare

Preparation Phase Checklist

The following table lists the steps necessary to complete the Preparation Phase for your website. Use this checklist to track your progress in this phase. The section that follows includes descriptions of each of the steps listed below.

Steps	Target Date	Completed Date
Identify a Product or Service		
Target an Audience		
Research Market and Competitors		
Define Return on Investment (ROI)		
Commit!		

Preparation Phase Description

There are endless opportunities for new businesses on the internet. Though the initial gold rush has passed for large companies, home-based businesses are now taking off. Due to the growth of affiliate programs, e.g. selling other people's products, there are many new opportunities for home-based businesses In this section, we discuss the steps involved in preparing to launch your online business. Simply put, you need to create a business plan for your internet business. We are not looking for a business plan worthy of a graduate thesis, but one that is simple and clearly defines the goals and objectives of your online business.

Identify a Product or Service

We do not go into a lengthy discussion on internet business ideas, because you probably already have an existing business or business idea that you want to develop on the internet. There are entire books and websites dedicated to online business opportunities. Before you continue with this guide, make sure you have a specific business or idea. Depending on your business, your website will serve a specific purpose. The typical business purposes for websites are listed below:

Brochure Site:

A Brochure Site is created to be an online marketing brochure for a brick and mortar operation. This type of site supports a product or service that is not easily delivered via the internet. Their "Call to Action" is to get a potential customer to call them or drive by. It is important for a Brochure Site to follow the same steps in this guide as an internet-only business, because more internet traffic ultimately leads to more phone calls or foot traffic.

Typical Brochure Sites: Construction Company, Restaurant, Day Care Provider

Direct Sales Site:

Direct sales sites provide a product or service that can be sold directly on the internet. Although the product or service may be delivered in person, the transaction occurs completely on the internet.

Example of Direct Product Site: Amazon.com

Example of a Direct Service Site: Elance.com

Combination Site:

Combination sites use their web pages both to market their brick and mortar stores as well as to sell products online. This approach has worked well for some companies but has failed miserably for others. Consider the recent failure of Borders bookstores.

Example of Combination Site: Sears.com

Affiliate Site:

Affiliate sites sell other people's products or services. In some cases, they perform the entire transaction and have the product shipped to the customer (drop shipping). In other cases, they are more of an advertising arm for the company.

Companies that offer affiliate programs: Amazon.com, Cafepress.com

Internet-Only Site:

Internet-only businesses may not actually sell anything or charge for anything. They create or host content that has value, which draws traffic to their website so that people pay them to host advertisements.

Examples of Internet-Only Businesses: Facebook.com, Google.com, Wikipedia.com, Cars.com

Speculative Site:

Speculative sites do not have any of their own content. They use SEO techniques to draw traffic to their site, hoping that someone will click on an ad or purchase a domain name at auction. Another type of Speculative Site is one that buys a misspelling or a domain name to get traffic. This type of site is questionable ethically.

There are new business models showing up (and disappearing) every day. By the time you read this, you may discover a new one.

What product or service are you going to provide?

_____

What type of website are you going to have?

_____

Target an Audience

One of the most exciting and explosive aspects of the internet is the ability to target very specific audiences. Through the internet, you have access to almost every age group, demographic, and geographic location in the world. Your idea will not fail because of your inability to find people. If you have a product or service that has value, your success will rely on your ability to get a visitor to perform an action. The action may be to make a purchase, pick up the phone, or click on an ad.

As with any business model, the ability to focus is essential on the internet. Your ability to focus not only helps you build a clear business model, but it also helps people find you. The best internet marketing campaigns focus on a very narrow marketing strategy. In this guide, we are going to imagine that Pam is launching a web site for a flower store in Plymouth, Massachusetts. This flower store provides flowers for every occasion and provides local delivery. Pam needs to focus her business model and marketing campaign very specifically. A Valentine's Day campaign in February to men between the ages of 18 and 50 is more effective than a year-round bouquet of roses campaign.

In addition to selecting your audience, you also want to select a single product line, piece of information, or teaser to be the primary focus of your internet marketing strategy.

Who is your target audience for your first campaign?

_____

What is your target product or service?

_____

We want to point out that one of the benefits of an online business is that you can make many mistakes at very little cost. Making changes to your audience or your product line is as simple as rewriting some content and changing some ads. If you want to start from scratch, it is still less expensive than opening a brick and mortar store. According to SBA.gov, "Seven out of 10 new employer firms last at least two years, and about half survive five years."[ii] The cost of failure is much lower with an internet business. The cost of success can be much higher because of the number of potential customers available on the internet.

Research Market and Competitors

One of the first steps in starting any business is analyzing your competitors and what they offer the marketplace. This is a relatively simple effort, yet many small businesses skip this step. Using the internet as a research tool has made this step easier. Answer the following question before you go any further:

When I type in my product or service on the top 3 search engines, what companies are showing up on the first few pages?

Once you have identified your competitors, complete the following
table for the top ten:

Company Name	Comparable Product or Service	Price/Offer
1.		
2.		
3.		
4.		
5.		
6.		
7.		
8.		
9.		
10.		

The best customer is the one you already have, which is true for
your competitors as well. People build up loyalty to companies
over time. When you are choosing a product or service, you should
plan to attract customers away from your competitors. Think
about how you will beat your competitors and then complete the
following sentences.

I will attract more customers to my website because:

_____.

Customers will likely leave my competitors because:

_____.

Define ROI

As with any business, it is critical to determine what you want your return on investment or ROI to be. Calculating ROI can be very complicated and can use complex formulas for inflation and interest. For our purposes, we want to make sure you are at least in the ballpark. Assuming you have built your site to make money, and it is not just a brochure site, answer the following questions:

Revenue Expectations

1. How much money do you have to invest?	
2. How long can you go without getting paid back?	
3. How much are you looking to make in Year 1?	
4. How much are you looking to make annually?	

Sales Expectation

1. How much will you sell one unit of your product for?	
2. How much profit do you expect to make on each sale, or transaction?	
3. How many transactions do you expect per month?	
4. Total Profit: Multiply #2 x #3 by 12 months *(This answer should be equal to or greater than answer #4 under Revenue Expectations.)*	

For those of you who are numbers people, this may be overly simplistic. In over 20 years of managing projects for large corporations, I have found that people do not look at the simple math and answer some simple questions when starting a project or business. Will we get our investment back if we do this project? How long will it take? Is this the best use of our money? How many items do I actually have to sell to meet my sales targets? So, keep these simple questions in mind as you launch your business, and do not assume that just because someone else is doing it, it is a good idea. Remember Borders bookstore.

If ROI is not critical to you, it is probably because your internet business does not need to make money immediately. In general, internet businesses usually fall into one of four categories:

- Hobbyist: a business model in which you can invest some time and a little money, and you do not need immediate payback of immediate revenue

- Franchisee: you are willing to pay someone else to help you build a solid business model

- Career Changer: you are going to apply all of your effort and patience to learning the business of internet marketing. You will make it succeed the same way you have in the traditional workplace.

- Innovator: you implemented an idea in which you had no intention of making money. You created a site, which had so much traffic it became profitable. Your idea was revolutionary; it was successful even though it lacked foresight or planning.

Notice that I did not use the term "entrepreneur" anywhere. This is an overused term. The stereotypical entrepreneur is perceived as a risk-taker with an all or nothing approach. If you are reading this book, you are an entrepreneur at heart, and you are trying to find a business model that makes you independent from the traditional work life. The level of risk associated with being an entrepreneur varies considerably from person to person.

✪ Important: Always underestimate your ROI. You do not have to be pessimistic. Just be realistic. Unless you have done this exact business model before, there will be a learning curve in order to meet your goals.

Commit!

The last step of the Preparation Phase it to Commit! Starting an online business is no easy feat. Though the cost in dollars to get started may be low, the cost in time, effort, and patience is high. The only way to succeed in business is to have a vision, a plan to accomplish it, and a commitment to complete the plan. Once you have started following the checklist, commit to completing it before you evaluate the success of your business model. Trying to lose weight, saving for a vacation, or starting a business all require the same things: a clear goal and a commitment for doing what it takes to achieve that goal. Start with a small goal first. Create a target date for each activity, one chapter at a time. Have some short-term wins to keep you motivated on the overall goals. This checklist, taken in totality, may seem overwhelming, so "chunk it up" into smaller pieces and perform one step at a time.

Chapter 3: Launch

Launch Phase Checklist

The following table lists the steps necessary to complete the Launch phase of your website. Use this checklist to track your progress in this phase. The section that follows includes descriptions of each of the steps listed below.

Steps	Target Date	Completed Date
Select Domain Name		
Generic Or Brand Names		
Brainstorming		
Domain Name Availability		
Associated Names		
Domain Name Registration		
Track Costs		
Select Hosting Company		
Determine Design Approach		
Determine Hosting Type		
Select Vendor & Track Cost		

Assign DNS To Domain Name		
Storyboarding		
Define All Content Pages		
Define Page Flow And Navigation		
Design Page Layouts		
Create Website		
Develop Home Page		
Upload And Review		
Expand Site		

Launch Phase Description

The Launch Phase explains the nuts and bolts of launching your website. Some of you may already have a website built. If so, review this section and determine if you followed these steps while launching your site, or if there are steps that you may have to go back and apply. We have learned this process through our own trial and error. Do not assume that if you made a decision that is different from what we suggest, you cannot go back and change. One of the wonderful things about an internet business is the low cost of entry and also the lower cost of change. Choosing a location for your brick and mortar business may be difficult to change once you have opened your doors, but changing your mind in the online world is much less costly and time consuming.

Select Domain Name

Selecting a domain name is the most important initial decision. Your domain name is the address you type into your web browser, e.g. www.yourdomainname.com. The selection of your domain name is critical because it establishes your brand on the internet.

Generic or Brand Names

There are two types of domain names you should consider when launching your website: generic names and brand names. Generic names use keywords, or descriptive words, as part of the name to help search engines and people identify the products or services you offer. For example:

www.CapeCodCarpentry.com

www.FunT-Shirts.com

www.Books.com

You understand what these businesses are offering by their domain name. In the examples above, the first two are also the company's names. The company names were selected at the same time as the domain name. Books.com is owned by Barnes and Noble and redirects to www.barnesandnoble.com. Barnes and Noble has saved untold millions in online marketing costs because anytime "book" is entered in a search engine, Barnes and Noble always shows up high in search results.

The use of a brand name for the domain name is important for companies with an established brand. For example:

www.Sears.com

www.Toyota.com

These businesses had an established brand long before the internet, and consumers know exactly what to enter to be directed to their site. Other companies select a unique brand name at the same time they launch their business. For example:

www.Amazon.com

www.GoDaddy.com

Both of these purely internet businesses have had tremendous success with their brand names despite the fact that their names are not descriptive of the products or services they offer. They have utilized many traditional advertising techniques to build their brand in addition to SEO techniques, but the quality of their products and services has ultimately led to their success.

As a new business, you need to decide whether or not you want a generic name or a brand name. There are pros and cons to each, and it is contingent to your overall branding strategy when choosing the type of domain name.

For Pam's fictitious flower store, we choose the generic domain name www.plymouthflowerstore.com. This domain name tells what she is offering and where it is located.

Brainstorming

One of the best techniques when selecting a business name or domain name is brainstorming. Webster's dictionary defines brainstorming as "a group problem-solving technique that involves the spontaneous contribution of ideas from all members of the group." Get with friends and/or family and discuss your ideas for your business name. Explain the differences between generic and brand names and allow them to weigh in. Remember, be open to all ideas; everyone is a consumer, and you will be surprised by the different feedback and ideas you receive.

The domain name I have chosen is _____.

Domain Name Availability

Once you have an idea for your domain name, you need to see if it is available. There are several sites that can tell you if a domain name is available. (See the Appendix for some suggested sites.) To see if your domain name is available, you enter it in the search box. There will be a listing of the domain name with every possible extension and an indication of whether or not it is available.

Many generic names may be taken with the .com extension, but if you really want the .com extension, consider adding a few additional letters such as "my" or your name to the domain name. There are an almost unlimited number of variations on domain names if you take this approach. For example, during the writing of this book, flowerstore.com was not available, but Plymouth-FlowerStore.com was available.

Also, if you really want a specific name and .com is not available, you can choose between several other extensions such as .org, net,

.co and others. .Com was intended for commerce sites, .org for non-profits, and .net of internet service providers (ISPs). There has not been any formal governance to prevent these extensions from being used for other purposes, so feel free to choose one of them instead. The extensions .edu (for education) and .gov (for US government) are two extensions that are regulated and off limits to businesses.

✪ **Important:** .co is now available as an alternative to .com. Time will tell if this extension will become as popular.

Associated Names

Once you have determined your domain name, you should simultaneously reserve, or sign up for, names that will support your networking efforts. Facebook® and Twitter® are two important services to get names associated with your domain name. You should also reserve your domain name with any blogs you may want to join. If you are not sure where else to reserve, review Chapter 6 for additional ideas.

We will discuss networking at length later on in this guide. However, you should now realize that, in order to increase the value of your brand, your implementation of these networking accounts will be built around your domain name, not your personal name.

Domain Name Registration

Once you have selected a domain name and have confirmed that it is available, your will have to register it. When you register a domain name, it is like renting a property with the option to renew every year. Once you register it, no one else can use it unless you choose not to renew it.

Domain names are controlled by ICANN (Internet Corporation for Assigned Names and Numbers). This not-for-profit organization oversees the registration of organizations that host domain names.

The list of accredited registrars can be found on ICANN's website at http://www.icann.org/en/registrars/accredited-list.html.

Myth: Domain name registration and website hosting have to be from the same company.

Fact: These two services are very different, and they can be provided from different companies.

Sometimes there are discounts available if you purchase both of these services from the same company. So, it is up to you whether or not to have both of these services from the same location. I use different providers for hosting and domain name registration in order to spread the risk of having all my eggs in one basket.

Domain registration generally costs $10.00 -$20.00 per year, depending on the package you purchase. If in doubt, purchase one year the first time. Then, you can add additional years when you renew.

(See the Appendix for a list of retail companies that offer domain name registration or refer to the ICANN website.)

Track Costs

○ **Important:** Domain name registration may be the first cost you incur in your new business. Though this expense is relatively small, get in the practice of tracking all costs, no matter how small. Businesses succeed (or fail) one dollar at a time.

Select Hosting Company

Selecting the host company sounds easier than it is. The company you choose will be an essential partner in your business, so you should not make a decision based solely upon price.

Development Approach

Before you select a hosting company, an important decision to make is how you are going to develop and publish your website. Though this decision can change, you initially need to decide how you want to develop your website; make sure the option you choose is supported by your hosting company. Your options range from full control--by coding and developing your site yourself--to minimal control-- by using a robust sitebuilder--along with options in between. The common options are as follows:

Outsource: The option that requires the least amount of technical knowledge or expertise is to outsource the development of your website to a 3rd party. There are two different options when choosing a 3rd party development partner. The first option is to hire a web development company. The second option is to hire a freelance developer to build your website. Now that Pam has grown her business, this is the approach she has been taking, along with using WordPress.

The fastest growing approach for finding freelance developers is hiring someone via the internet that may live and work anywhere in the world. This option gives you a significant cost reduction over hiring a local company. Website designers on these sites are plentiful and affordable. Website design is a commodity item now, so you can shop around. Once you have selected a designer based upon cost and review of their portfolio, the best approach for working with them is to find a site that you like the look and feel of, and provide that site as an example of what you are looking for. (See the Appendix for a list of website development resources.)

Sitebuilders: This is the next easiest option. In this option, you select a template from your hosting provider and type in your content as if you were working on a word processor. You do not need to be technical at all. If you are choosing this option, make sure you see the choice of templates provided by your hosting company prior to purchasing.

WordPress: WordPress is currently the most popular approach for start-ups. It provides you some of the ease of a sitebuilder by providing customizable templates, while allowing more technical modifications to be made by you or a developer.

CSS or other Templates: Even if you are interested in building your own site using a development tool such as Dreamweaver® or Microsoft's Expression Web®, it is still easier and faster to start with a template. There are CSS (cascading style sheet) templates that provide you with a layout, look, and feel, so that when you create any new page based upon that template, it will have the same look and feel as the home page. There are full site templates which have all the pages of a standard website and that just need to be customized. Depending what you are looking for, the internet is full of well-designed templates ranging in price anywhere from free to a few hundred dollars. These templates give you a jump start on designing your website.

Full Custom: If you have the technical knowhow, time, and desire, creating your own custom site gives you the most control. Though it will take longer to create than starting with a template, you will know every piece of the website. If there are any changes or modifications you want to make, you can do them quickly and easily. With the prior options, changes or customizations can sometimes take too much time, which could potentially impact sales or cause you to miss an opportunity.

As with anything else in life, you need to know your strengths and weaknesses in order to "play to your strengths." If you are some-one who has previously taken advanced classes in Photoshop® or desktop publishing, it will not be a stretch to learn a development tool. If you have difficulty getting the clock to stop blinking on your VCR, you may want to stick with a sitebuilder or go with outsourced development. Regardless of your choice, you will have to develop some technical knowhow if you want to run an online business. You will at least need to get comfortable with all of the terminology regarding this business model so that you can communicate effectively with your partners.

The development approach I will be using is _____.

Determine Hosting Type

Hosting companies specialize in different types of hosting. Some of the things to consider when selecting a hosting company are:

Free Hosting: Yes, it is true; there are companies that will host your websites for free. Usually free hosting requires that you allow the companies to include advertising on your page. If you are just trying a proof of concept or hobby page, free hosting might be an acceptable approach.

Reliability: If your site is down, you do not make money. Therefore, it is important to find a reliable site. Make sure your site is rated by a 3rd party to have an up-time of 99% or better.

Dedicated or Shared Servers: The standard offering from hosting companies is to put you on the same physical server or computer as other customers. This works fine for most websites. If you do not want to share a physical location with other websites because of the secure nature of your information, or the need for the highest performance possible, you can pay a premium price to have a dedicated server.

Number of Domains Names: If you are planning to have multiple websites, make sure the package you select will allow you to host multiple sites for one flat fee. It will get costly if you pay for hosting for each website.

Email: Most hosting companies will provide email that uses your domain name at no extra charge. You can usually use their online e-mail applications to check and send mail, or you can set them up to work with applications such as Outlook® or on your iPhone®.

Shopping Cart: If you are planning to sell products from your website, you will need to select a package that includes a Shopping Cart and SSL (secure socket layer), which provides for secure transactions. You do not have to use the shopping cart from your hosting company; you can also interact with third party payment systems such as PayPal® or Google Checkout®.

Development Tools: If you are choosing a custom or outsourced development approach, make sure the hosting company allows you to upload custom websites. If they say they offer *FTP* (file transfer protocol) it means they provide the ability to upload a custom site that you have created.

Select Vendor

Unfortunately, hosting companies are a dime a dozen. There are literally thousands to choose from. Some are small shops that are run by a single person; some are large but overpriced or have antiquated tools. This is one area in which you have to shop around, read reviews, and dig a little deeper. In the Appendix, we have listed some vendors that we have worked with. Be a good consumer and find the right fit for you. Typical plans range from $5.00 - $20.00 per month. You should not need to pay any more than that.

✪ **Important:** Some additional considerations are the number of years on the contract, payment plans, and discounts. Once you have selected a vendor and paid for the service, be sure you track your costs.

Assign DNS to Domain Name

Your DNS (domain name system) is similar to your street address for your domain name. The DNS tells the internet where to go to find your domain name. Your hosting company is the neighborhood. Once the internet gets to the neighborhood, the hosting company has a list of all the domains, and it points the internet directly to your house, or in this case, your domain name and web page. If you purchased your domain name at the same company as your hosting package, you do not have to worry about this. If not, you need to perform the following steps.

When you purchase your hosting package, one of the first things you will get from them--usually in your confirmation email--is their DNS information. The information will look something like this:

```
1st Nameserver: ns170.hostingcompany.com

2nd Nameserver: ns171.hostingcompany.com
```

This information needs to be entered with the company where you registered your domain name. All companies have a different protocol, but you will probably just need to login to your domain name company and find a setting for managing your DNS. It will be clear where to enter your new DNS information. Once you enter that information, your domain name will be assigned to your hosting company and should show up in your browser in an hour or so, but usually no more than 24 hours.

Storyboarding

The term storyboarding refers to the movie industry technique for drawing different scenes in advance to help layout the plot and sequence of events in a movie or film. In website design, it has a similar purpose. The purpose is to lay out what content you want in your site and to draw a picture of how you want your customer to navigate your site. The storyboarding steps I use when designing a website are as follows:

Define all content pages

I first list the main topic areas and pages that I want to create in my site, for example:

- Home Page

- Products

- Services

- About Us

- My Blog

- Contact Us

- Etc.

Define Page Flow and Navigation

Then I create a diagram of how I want the site to be organized and how I want navigation to occur:

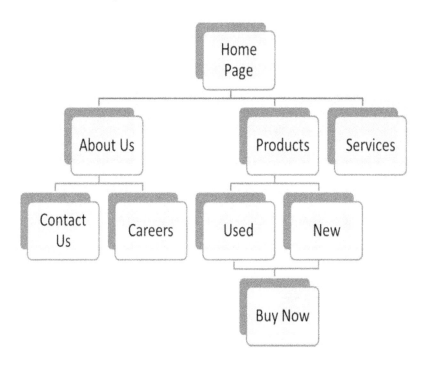

Design Page Layouts

The last step is to design the format of each page. A typical format for a home page is as follows:

Header/Banner/Logo/ Company Name	
Navigation 1 2 3….	Content Area 1
	Content Area 2…..
Footer, copyright, additional navigation…	

Having your layout determined in advance will help you rapidly develop your website or help you communicate with a development partner. The home page may have a different look and feel than your subpages, but do not create too many formats because it will be harder to maintain as you grow your site or if you want to make changes.

Create Website

Develop Home Page

Now the fun begins! Once you have selected your development approach and determined your content and layout, you are ready to build your website. The first step is to create the content for your home page. Based upon your storyboard, you have determined the pages you want and navigation, so you can populate your menu. Next, you need to populate your homepage by including standard items such as logo, company name, and tagline. The next step is to document any informational content.

Upload and Review

Once you have created the homepage, work with your hosting company to publish that first page. Depending on the development approach you took, this could be as simple as pressing a "publish" button or as complicated as a few hours configuring your tool and the FTP settings. There are many different ways to publish, so we will not go into them all here. There are always straightforward tutorials that are provided by hosting companies to walk you through this process. Be patient and do not let the terminology intimidate you.

This step serves two purposes. The first is to get you comfortable with the upload process because you will be doing it frequently. The second is to validate your look and feel before you go too far. This is very important on sitebuilder sites and WordPress sites because the published version can look very different from the development screen on which you have been working. This is the easiest time to make substantial changes to your site. A well-designed site can be updated relatively easy later on, but major structural changes are always hard to make once your site has grown and you have many pages and content. So, take your time and get it right.

Expand Site

Once you are satisfied with your look and feel, you can start to create the rest of the pages in your site.

✪ **Important:**   Before you create any additional pages, read the next chapter of this guide in order to understand and begin to apply some of the key SEO design elements while you are building your pages. You could always go back later and do this, but if you are able to apply some of these techniques as you build it the first time, it will make the process a little easier.

Another suggestion I have is to publish the site each time you create a page. That way you can test the navigation and validate that you have not broken anything. This approach assumes that you have not marketed your website yet. You do not want your customers coming to your site and seeing it in disarray. The reason I suggest this approach is that many features of a website may not work if you only run it on your computer. If you are developing the site yourself, the only way to truly see if it is working is to have it running at the hosting company.

Chapter 4: Optimize

Optimization Phase Checklist

The following table lists the steps necessary to complete the Optimization Phase of your website. Use this checklist to track your progress in this phase. The sections that follow include descriptions of each of the steps listed below.

Steps	Target Date	Completed Date
Identify Keywords		
Keyword Research		
Keyword Definition		
Populate Meta Tags		
Title		
Description		
Keywords		
Robots		
Apply Keywords		
Title		
Content		
Headings, H1, H2, H3...		

Strong, <Em>, <B>		
Image Attributes		
Anchor Text		
Build Content		
Validate Keyword Use		
Semantic Latent Indexing		
Associate Content With Media		
Create Unique Content		
Set A Schedule To Maintain		
Optimize Navigation Structure		
# Of Levels		
Breadcrumbs		
Page And Path Names		
Images In Menu		
Absolute URLs		
Create Conversion Strategy		
Identify Call To Action		
Modify Site To Apply		
Ensure Approach Is Trackable		
Review For Poor Design		

Optimization Phase Description

Now that you have built your website, I know you want to learn how to grow your business using Facebook® or Twitter® by connecting to Friends and Tweeting. You have probably read about all the fun things you can do to grow your business in this day and age. What you do not hear about very often are the building blocks that need to be in place in order to take advantage of those fun opportunities. We will definitely spend time on the "fun stuff" in the next chapter, but this chapter is about building a solid foundation for your website so that the walls do not crumble when you add all the weight of social marketing and advertising.

In the Optimization Phase, we will explain the techniques you need to use to create a search-engine friendly site. This chapter will focus on how to create a site that is easy to navigate and clearly presents content to visitors and search engines—content that ensures your visitors understand the purpose and value of your site and keeps them coming back

Identify Keywords

A keyword or keyword phrase is a descriptive word or descriptive phrase used by search engines to find relevant websites. You began identifying keywords in the preparation phase, and you will continue to evolve your keywords throughout the life of your business. We define the importance of keywords now, but we will expand upon their use throughout the chapter.

When you were brainstorming for your domain name, you probably began brainstorming keywords. You may have even chosen your domain name to include keywords, for example www.plymouthflowerstore.com versus www.flowershizzle.com (pardon my attempt to be hip). Consistently-used and strategically-placed keywords within the content of your site are the backbone of a well optimized site.

Keyword Research: The identification of keywords for your site is straightforward. There are presently many tools to identify what keywords are associated with particular terms or even what keywords are associated with your competitors. The most common one is Google's keyword tool which can be found in the Appendix along with other keyword resources. This tool is designed to support Google's AdWords® product, but is also free for anyone to use for keyword research. For example, if I want to see the most common searches for a local Flower Store, I enter the phrase "Flower Store in Plymouth." The top keywords used in Google are *florist, flowers in, bouquet,* and more.

You can also use this tool to see what keywords your competitors are using. If you type in www.flowers.com as your competitor's website, you will see similar and additional keywords that are being used by FTD.com.

Keyword Definition: Once you perform keyword research, you will learn which words are important to include in your website. This is critical if you want Google to categorize you similarly to your competitors, or to appropriately align your site with the products or services you sell.

Make a list of the top 10-20 keywords that you want to make sure you include in your design and content:

1.	2.	3.	4.	5.
6.	7.	8.	9.	10.
11.	12.	13.	14.	15.
16.	17.	18.	19.	20.

Populate Meta Tags

Part of the information that search engines read in your website is captured in *meta tags*. Meta tags are invisible to visitors in the browser but are critical to SEO. In order to understand meta tags, you need to understand a little about the underlying structure of a web site. Websites were originally written solely in HTML (hypertext markup language). Although there are many additional development components of websites, such as java, xml, css, the basic structure of an HTML webpage is as follows:

```
<!DOCTYPE html>

<html>

  <head>

    <title>The Plymouth Flower Store</title>

  </head>

  <body>

    <p>My content</p>

  </body>

</html>
```

A website design can be as simple as that. The above HTML code will produce an actual web page. There are areas in the code shown above that you modify to add content. Everything between <head> and </head> is called the *header*, and everything between <body> and </body> is called, yes, you guessed it, the *body*. In the following section we focus on the header.

The header contains a great deal of content in which search engines are interested. This information is mostly invisible to the webpage visitor, but the header defines information about your site and how search engines should interpret your site. It includes everything from the version of HTML you are using to the title and description you have. We will not go over all of the options for the header. We have chosen those which are most commonly edited by you or your developer.

✪ **Important:** Did you know you can view the meta tags of any website you are visiting? Go to menu of your browser and click on View, Source to open a document which will show the meta tags and actual content behind the webpage.

Note: Even if you are using a sitebuilder or WordPress and not touching the actual code, the elements that follow are often filled in as part of your web site creation process in an online form.

Title:

```
<title>content</title>
```

Though title is not technically a meta tag, it is an element that resides in the header and is visible in the title bar at the top of the browser. The title is also the content that the search engine displays when it shows your site in search results. The title should be no more than 60 characters long and should represent the content on the page. On the homepage, the title should be the name of your company. We will explain later the content of the title on subpages.

Description:

```
<meta name="description" content="your descrip-
tion here" />
```

The description meta tag is used by browsers to populate the description on the search engine results. Experts believe that most search engines do not use this for SEO, but only for presenting information. This impacts SEO in that a well-written description is important to draw visitors to your site. We recommend that the description contain no more than 160 characters.

Bad description:

We are a Flower Store that delivers flowers in Plymouth.

Good description:

Plymouth's premier Flower Store with a 99.9% on time delivery rate.

✪ **Important:** The description is a key marketing component of your SEO plan. It is important to deploy it successfully as soon as you launch your site.

Keywords:

```
<meta name="keywords" content="flowers, delivery
in Plymouth, roses, wedding bouquets"/>
```

Once, this was the most important meta tag in the header. The keywords meta tag is now ignored by Google and is of lower importance to other search engines. Its overuse and abuse have removed it from the critical element that it once was. That is not to say you should not populate it. Who is to say what search engine your customer is using? It does not take significant effort to populate. We recommend no more than 150 characters and no more than fifteen keywords or keyword phrases.

Robots:

```
<meta name="robots" content="syntax">
```

Robots is a more advanced meta tag which is not necessarily populated by site builders or other templates. The purpose of the robots tag is to tell search engines what to do when they are crawling your site. The two most common syntaxes of the robots elements are:

noindex: tells search engines not to include that page in their search results. Usually this is used for incomplete pages, advertising landing pages, or low-value pages such as a search page. The assumption is that you only want search engines to crawl high-value pages so that it gives your overall site a high ranking

nofollow: tells search engines not to follow any links on the page. You may use this if the links are often subject to change.

Apply Keywords

Until this point you have been creating the foundation for your website and ensuring you have created something that is visually pleasing. This is where many website developers stop because they either are not trained in SEO, or they were not hired to optimize the website. Their only concern was to create a site that is nice looking or user-friendly.

✪ **Important:** The application of keywords to your website is a critical component of SEO. It tells the search engine that your message is clear and that visitors to your site will see quality information related to the search term they entered.

Title

Modifying the title is a newer approach in improving your SEO. The home page title should include the company name in the first page, but all subpages should be changed to include keywords that represent the content of that specific page. Since the keyword element and description are not used to categorize a page by the search engine, the titles are now part of the categorization of a page.

Bad example:

Order Form Page

Good Example:

Secure Online Ordering Form for Flower Delivery in Plymouth.

This example applies specific keywords to the page and is the content that will be at the top of the browser. If you leave the title the same on every page, such as Plymouth Flower Store, then this can be interpreted by search engine as "duplicate content" which may negatively impact the ranking of that page.

🖐 **Warning:** Search engines will penalize you if you are repeating content throughout your site. Do not post copies of your blogs on multiple pages or repeat your advertising and marketing on every page. Search engines look for unique content when ranking web pages.

Headings, H1, H2, H3...

Now we are going to describe attributes of the content in the *Body* of your website. You may not realize it, but HTML has standard formatting for titles and headings in your pages. If you understand word processing, then you know you can set a font to a specific size, such as 11pt. In HTML, headings are defined by relative sizes such as x-large, large, medium, and small. The tags for those headings, <H1>, <H2>, <H3>, etc., are wrapped around your text to show the relative size of headings and subheadings and to differentiate the headings from standard paragraph fonts in the body of your HTML. <H1> headings are typically the largest fonts on the web page. The actual size of these headings are determined by the browser settings or by your web design style sheets.

Search engines will pay extra attention to the content within these heading tags when identifying what your site is about. The <H1> heading is usually at the top of each page and is the most important. It should be both descriptive of the page and include keywords when possible.

Bad heading: <H1>About Us</H1>

Good heading: <H1> About Plymouth's Flower Store – The best quality flower arrangements in Plymouth, MA. </H1>

<H1> headings should only be used once on each page, unless you want to be penalized for keyword stuffing. Keyword stuffing is the overuse or hiding of numerous keywords. For example, sentences that tell people that you are a flower expert who went to flower school and studied flowers so you could start a flower store not only will annoy your visitors, but may also be considered keyword stuffing.

☛ **Warning:** Keyword stuffing can get you penalized or banned by search engines.

<strong>, <em>, <b>

Keywords in the *Body* of your site can also be emphasized for search engines based upon how you format them. In HTML, the codes <strong>, <em>, <b> are wrapped around words to show words in **bold** on your site. These bold attributes should call attention to keywords that you want to emphasize for your visitor. Search Engines will conclude that this information is more important if it is in bold and will help them categorize your site.

Example: The Plymouth Flower Store has a <strong> Valentine's Day Special.</strong> is displayed as The Plymouth Store has a **Valentine's Day Special**.

✪ **Important:** **Do not** overuse **this** feature, **because it** can be **annoying** to the **reader** ☺

Alt Image Attribute

Another newer SEO strategy to display keywords involves completing the *Alt* element of images on your website. The *Alt* Attribute is a label that is assigned to every image on your website. Back in the "old days," we always populated this content with the name of the image. That is because web pages were so slow to load, you did not want to wait to see what the page was about, so you could read the image label. With high-speed internet, the practice was almost discontinued. Now, due to SEO and accessibility considerations, *Alt* is once again being populated with more robust content.

Bad example:

```
<img src="logo.png" alt="Company Logo">
```

Good example :

```
<img src="Plymouth_Flower_Store_logo.png" alt=
"The logo for the best Flower Store in Plymouth">
```

✪ **Important:** Most website development tools and WordPress will now prompt you to fill in the *Alt* Attribute information when you insert an image in your website.

Anchor Text

An important approach for SEO is the use of keywords in anchor text. Anchor text is the label that is associated with a link or hyperlink to a web page. Instead of seeing www.plymouth-flowerstore.com on a webpage, you often just see Plymouth's Flower Store and the URL or website name is hidden.

✪ **Important:** Search engines find anchor text more important than regular text, so it is a good practice to include keywords for your hyperlinks.

Bad example:

To learn more about our delivery options, <u>Click Here</u>

Good Example:

Follow this link to learn more about our <u>on-time delivery guarantee.</u>

Build Content

The content on your site is its most valuable asset both for your visitors and for search engines. Presenting high-quality, fresh content on your website is very important. Better content will keep visitors on your site longer. Fresh content is also considered by search engines to be an important component of ranking. When search engines crawl your site, they are able to identify if the content has been updated. Updating your website informs the search engine that you provide up-to-date and valuable content to your visitors.

Validate Keyword Use

As we mentioned previously, try to keep your content consistent with your keyword strategy. Do not make your homepage all about wedding bouquets if your specialty is local flower delivery. On a reverse note, do not overdo the use of keywords. Recall our earlier discussion about the risk of keyword stuffing.

Semantic Latent Indexing

Semantic Latent Indexing is a fancy SEO term for using synonyms. Potential visitors and search engines will categorize your site based upon search terms, which may not be initially apparent to you, but which are common. You may call your site Plymouth's Flower Store, but many people still refer to flower stores as florists. Performing Semantic Latent Indexing is as simple as using a thesaurus such as http://synonyms.memodata.com/ and typing in your keywords. For example, when I type in florist, I get the following:

> floriculturist, florist's shop, florist shop, flower-grower, Flower Store, flower stand, flower store, florist's *(ellipsis)*, flower stall *(spéc. anglais britannique)*

These synonyms can all be part of your content and keyword strategy.

Associate Content with Videos

If you are going to include video on your site, do not put it on a page all by itself. If a search engine crawls a page with only videos and no content, it will assume it has little value and will not rank it very high. You should always include content on the page that describes the video. Some people put complete transcriptions of the video content on the page. This rule also applies to having only images on a page.

✎ **Warning:** Do not use graphics or videos as your primary messaging tool. Otherwise, search engines will devalue those pages.

Create Unique Content

Content is king! Make sure that you produce content-rich pages. Be an authority for users by producing excellent content. If it is appropriate to your business, be an expert. Provide valuable information as part of your website, and you will drive more traffic to your site for that reason alone. Blogging is one way to create quality content. Other ways to create fresh content include: product reviews, customer testimonials, and employee profiles. For example, for Plymouth's Flower Store, we could include content on how to keep your flowers alive longer, or the historical significance of different flowers as gifts.

Set a schedule to maintain

As part of the ongoing maintenance of your website, you will be updating and refreshing your content. At this point in your SEO plan, you should create a schedule to manage your content. Whether it be daily, weekly, or monthly you should create a specific plan completing your content updates. As we say in project management, you cannot manage what you cannot measure. So, create the schedule now, and you can measure your effectiveness later.

If you are not already doing this, create a calendar--either electronically or on paper--which logs your key start-up and maintenance activities with actual dates. As with any successful business, clear, defined goals are a key part of your strategy.

✪ **Important:** Make your goals S.M.A.R.T: Specific, Measureable, Achievable, Realistic, and Timely.

Define Navigation Structure

Having a simple and clear navigation structure is important to search engines and visitors. Navigation is considered more important to users than design or look and feel. Search engines use your navigation to index your site. If a link is broken, it will not be indexed. If your navigation is confusing, the search engine will penalize you. If your navigation is clear and the site can be crawled easily, you may be fortunate enough for Google to show your *sitelinks*.

Sitelinks are a nice feature of Google's but they are difficult to guarantee. From Google's Webmaster Forum[iii]:

"We only show sitelinks for results when we think they'll be useful to the user. If the structure of your site does not allow our algorithms to find good sitelinks, or we do not think that the sitelinks for your site are relevant for the user's query, we will not show them."

For example, see the associated sitelinks for my son's site, www.capecodcarpentry.com.

Navigation is important for visitors because it helps them know where they are and where they are going, and, hopefully, supports whatever action you are expecting. Simple tips include keeping navigation all in one area on the page, preferably somewhere near the top on the screen. There can be links to less important content elsewhere within the page, but the key, action-driven navigation should be combined and put in the same place on the homepage and all subpages.

of Levels

All of the pages within your site should be reached within three levels. Level 1 is your homepage; level 2 are linked to your homepage; and level 3 are linked to level 2. Any levels below that will lose visitors and cause confusion. Call to Actions should be within 2 levels from a landing page.

☛ **Warning:** Every time visitors have to click on another page increases the chance that they will leave your site.

Breadcrumbs

Breadcrumbs is a way to design your navigation so that you always show your visitors where they are and where they came from. This is useful both to the visitor and search engine. A simple example is:

Plymouth's Flower Store > Holiday Bouquets > Valentine's Day > **Roses**

The use of breadcrumbs is very common on large product sites where not only do you need to know where you are, but you may want to navigate back a couple of places along your path. Many people in the industry believe that this approach reduces the percentage of people who will leave your site prematurely.

Page and Path Names

Some Sitebuilders including WordPress default the names of new pages to something that does not make sense to a visitor. For example, you may have seen a URL that looks like http://plymouthflow-erstore.com/56874/?p=123. These types of path names or page names are confusing to visitors and search engines. A search engine may have an easier time indexing this page if the path and page name are clearer. Also, if keywords are in the path name, they will improve your SEO.

WordPress can be reconfigured to change the default page naming convention. Most of the other development approaches allow you to define the name of the subpage. I like to use a – or _ as part of the file name such as holiday_bouquets.htm. It makes it easier for search engines to separate the names into keywords, and it is friendlier for visitors.

Images in Menu

Often, web designers want to have fancy icons or pictures as part of the menu. This is a big problem for a search engine that is trying to understand how to navigate your site. The search engine will only see links to pictures without realizing that the primary navigation is being listed there. This will also prevent search engines like Google from optimizing your search results and providing user-friendly sitelinks.

Absolute URLs

Many designers and tools create internal links using relative URLs. Relative URLs are hyperlinks, which show only where you are going relative to the page you are currently on. For example, if you are on a home page and you click on the Product menu item, the associated link may only be /product.html.

HTML is smart, and it recognizes that if you are on the home page of Plymouthflowerstore.com, and you click on a link that is coded /products.html, you really want to go to: www.plymouthflowerstore.com/products.html.

So, "What is the problem?" you ask. The SEO "experts" cannot come to a consensus on this one, but most experts believe that having the full or "absolute" URL for every link such as www.plymouthflowerstore.com/products.html cannot hurt SEO and may help search engines crawling your site. In addition, if someone has copied your content, either ethically or unethically, any links within the content will point you back to your site.

Create Conversion Strategy

All the work you have done up to this point is wasted if you do not get your visitors to become customers. The purpose of your website and your SEO plan should be pre-defined, based upon your business model. It is seldom enough to get someone just to show up to your website. You most likely want them to perform some action.

Construct the Call to Action

For the purpose of this guide, I will assume that your website is being created to make money. Based upon this assumption the basic Call to Actions are:

- Get a visitor to become a customer by buying a product or service from you. This is a direct sale action. Amazon and Zappos® are successful businesses with this model.

- Get visitor to click on a link that has them buying a product or service from someone with whom you are an affiliate. This is a Pay Per Sale (PPS) action. Affiliating with Zazzle and Café Press are successful business models.

- Provide advertising on your website. This is a Pay Per Click (PPC) action. The bulk of revenues for Facebook® and Google® come from selling PPC advertising. If you have a high volume traffic site, this is the most common way to generate revenue.

✿ **Warning:** There are pay per lead and pay per click affiliate programs that have become abused and unethical – be wary and do your research before you get involved with any of these firms.

As we mentioned in Chapter 2 of this guide, you may also be creating your website as a marketing brochure for your brick and mortar business. Even if you are not generating income online, you may still want a conversion approach that keeps the customer on your site so that they are more likely to return and also will visit your location. Examples are:

- **Coupons, discounts, specials**: Create an online coupon that keeps visitors coming back to your website.

- **Surveys**: Some people love taking surveys. Create one that has your customer being more interested in your product or service.

- **Videos**: A fun, embedded video, or link to a YouTube® video can hook a visitor to staying on your site and will begin the process of creating a brand and customer loyalty.

Modify Site

In order to implement your conversion strategy, you have to modify the site to help guide the visitor toward your desired action. The Call to Action should be no more than two levels deep. For example, the link on which a customer clicks to buy a product should be at the home page or on a page that is linked to the homepage. The distance (# of clicks) from the homepage is directly related to the percentage of visitors who leave your site or perform a Call to Action. The Call to Action should be placed higher up on the page so that the visitor does not have to scroll down to see it.

You may have to play around with different designs and see the results before you find one that works. This is the "art" of SEO and requires patience and flexibility.

Review for poor design

The last component to optimize your website is to review it for poor design. Key elements of a poor SEO design are as follows:

Keyword Stuffing: Even though we do not know the magic number, we do know that search engines will penalize your site if you have too many of the same keywords near each other. Think of yourself as a visitor when you are reviewing your content. Remember, the search engines are built by people who are attempting to have the search engines view your site as a visitor. So, focus on clear, concise content with synonyms and the appropriate use of your keywords.

Flash Intro Pages: Have you ever been to a site where the first thing you see is a beautiful slide show showing you all their products and services? Well, that is most likely developed in Adobe® Flash®, and a search engine has no idea what it is on that page. Remember, web site design and SEO are not the same thing, and sometimes they even compete with each other.

Flash is still popular with many designers. It creates a great visual experience for the visitor, and it can portray a level of profession-alism. That being said, Flash cannot be read by search engines.

Use Flash sparingly to complement your content. Once you have steady traffic to your site and you want to "fancy it up" then add Flash, but remember: the most important aspect of SEO is for search engines to find you.

Too many videos or images: As with Flash, search engines cannot read images or video. We discussed previously the ways to associate content with these components. If you look at a web page and more than one-third of the page is covered by images or video, you are not optimizing the real estate on your web site effectively.

✪ **Important:** Use a tool to evaluate the effectiveness of the SEO design of your website. There are both commercial and free tools that perform this function. (See the Appendix for a list of SEO analysis tools.)

Chapter 5: Submit

Submission Phase Checklist

The following table lists the steps necessary to complete the Submission phase for your website. Use this checklist to track your progress in this phase. The sections that follow include descriptions of each of the steps listed below.

Steps	Target Date	Completed Date
Submit Sites		
Submit Site to Google		
Submit Site to Yahoo		
Submit Site to Bing		
Submit XML Sitemaps		
Create SiteMap		
Submit SiteMap to Google		
Submit SiteMap to Yahoo		
Submit SiteMap to Bing		
Automate SiteMap		
Build Links		
Create a Plan		

Buying Links		
Submit to Directories		
Validate Link Building "Don'ts"		

Submission Phase Description

The Submission Phase is the first time you are proactively inform-
ing search engines and the rest of the internet that you have
arrived. Until this point, you have been preparing your site to be
viewed. Now, you will officially notify search engines of your
presence.

The biggest benefit of this phase is its impact on the speed with
which your site gets *indexed*. To be *indexed* just means that
Google has you on their list of websites that could show up in
search results. Through experience, we have found that this phase
makes the most dramatic short-term impact on SEO and your
search engine results position (SERP).

Submit Sites

Each Search Engine has a different approach to submitting your
URL to them. The good news is that you only have to submit your
site once for each search engine.

Submit Site to Google®

Go to Google Webmaster Tools, http://www.google.com/web-
masters/. Click on Sign In, and if you do not have a Gmail®
account, create one. At the home page, click on Add a Site. Google
will give you two options: the Recommended method and the
Alternative method. The Recommended method asks you to
download a file from Google and put it in the same folder as your
home page. The Alternative method asks you to add some information to the header of your homepage. Your development
method will likely determine which method you should choose. If
you have access to the HTML on your site, I would suggest the
Alternative method because it will also support your tracking
approach.

Once you perform either approach, click on Verify, and Google will confirm verification. Once you have completed that, there is nothing else to do. It usually takes a few days for Google to index all of your pages once it has been verified. You can check back with Google to see if the indexing is complete.

Submit Site to Yahoo®

Similar to Google, go to Yahoo's webmaster tool, Site Explorer at http://siteexplorer.search.yahoo.com/ and login or create a Yahoo account. (Yes, you will have many more email accounts now that you are an internet businessperson.) Once you are in Site Explorer, you can click Submit your Site and you are done. Your site is submitted to the index. If you want to eventually use any other of the analytic or tracking features of Site Explorer, you will need to perform the similar actions as Google: upload a file or add a snippet of code to your header in your homepage.

Submit Site to Bing®

Access the Bing's webmaster Toolbox at http://www.bing.com /toolbox/webmaster to login or create a Windows® LiveID® account if you do not already have one. Click on Add Site, and it will ask you to perform similar steps as Google. You cannot get indexed with Bing without the verification process complete. Bing seems to be the slowest to complete the indexing process. It can take months to have all of your pages indexed on Bing.

Submit XML Site Maps

Once you have submitted your sites, you can provide the search engines with another important piece of SEO information about your site: an XML site map. An XML site map is a file that tells the search engine the structure of your site and helps them understand how to crawl through it. It is not required, but it increases your SEO and could help create sitelinks under your search results.

If you are curious what one looks like, go to any site and type in sitemap.xml at the end of the URL, such as www.seomanifesto.com/sitemap.xml.

Create SiteMap.xml

To create a site map, you can use the free tools listed in the Appendix. The following describes the approach at http://www.sitemapdoc.com/. Go to the site, enter your URL, and click enter. Once the process is complete, you may see several different versions of site maps. Click on the one that says sitemap.xml and save it to your computer. You will then need to copy that document to the same folder at your hosting company as your homepage (or have your developer do it for you). Once you have created it the first time, the next step is to submit the site map to each search engine.

Submit SiteMap to Google

Go to Google Webmaster Tools, http://www.google.com/webmasters/, sign in, and go to the Dashboard. Once there, click on Site Configuration, and then Sitemaps, and type sitemap.xml in the box. Click Submit Sitemap.

Submit SiteMap to Yahoo

Go to Site Explorer, http://siteexplorer.search.yahoo.com/ and sign in. Click on My Sites and then click on your URL. Then click on Feeds. Enter sitemap.xml into the box, leave option as Web Site Feed, and click on Add Feed.

Submit SiteMap to Bing

Go to http://www.bing.com/toolbox/webmaster Go to the Crawl tab and select Sitemaps (XML, Atom, RSS) on the top menu. Click on Add Feed, and type in sitemap.xml in the box. Click on Submit.

✪ **Important:** Site Maps should be submitted anytime you add, remove, or rename a page on your site. The good news is that some hosting companies and development tools can be configured to automatically submit these for you.

Submit Links

The most successful, yet most abused, method of improving your SEO over the long term is link submission. Search engines look at the quantity and quality of links coming to your site from other web pages as a key part of their ranking algorithm. They are assuming that your content is so pertinent, valuable, and interesting that other pages are putting links to you on their websites. These links are called backlinks. Since this is still a critical component of their ranking strategy, search engines are keeping this as a key criterion. At the same time, they are severely penalizing those sites that abuse it.

Link Quality

Search engines look at the type of sites to which you are linked in order to evaluate the quality of the link. Directories are higher quality links. A quick way to determine the quality of site is by viewing their Google PageRank®. We will discuss PageRank further in Chapter 8, but in the meantime, suffice to say, Google's PageRank tool scores a site on a 10-point scale and will give you a relative quality of a site.

Linking to directories

An ethical and practical approach to linking is to link to directories. Directories are repositories of web pages, not much different than telephone books were at one time. They collect information about your web site including a description. They will also typically categorize you by industry and location. There are some massive directories that house many of the web sites in the internet.

Unfortunately, some of them charge money. Here are some of the most popular:

Dmoz.org – PageRank of 8 out of 10: Free

Yahoo Directory –PageRank of 8 out of 10: $299 per year

Best of the Web –PageRank of 7 out of 10: $99 per year

Business.com - PageRank of 5 out of 10: $299 per year

Pam, who is extremely successful with her SEO approach, does not use any of the paid directory services. We believe that the best directories to link to are those that are in your industry. For example, Plymouth's Flower Store could register with an industry florist directory, LocalFlorist.com with a PageRank of 3 for $149 per year. That would create a backlink and would also provide some industry specific advertising.

Review what your competitors are linking to if you want to see what the most common backlinks are. Later on, we will discuss different ways to identify backlinks of any website. Most of these techniques can be run against your competitors' websites so that you can see what sites they are linking to.

Link Building Don'ts

Since misuse or abuse can penalize you, it is important to know some of the unethical approaches to building links that you should avoid.

Buy Poor Quality Links from Link Farms: Links Farms are terms for websites or number of websites that charge you to post your URL but provide no other value. These sites will ultimately get banned from search engines and will hurt your ranking.

Create too many links too quickly: Creating more than a few hundred a day will negatively impact your site because a search engine will assume that you are engaging in a link scam.

Chapter 6: Network

Networking Phase Checklist

The following table lists the steps necessary to complete the Networking phase for your website. Use this checklist to track your progress in this phase. The section that follows includes descriptions of each of the steps listed below.

Steps	Target Date	Completed Date
Create Plan And Approach		
Utilize Facebook®		
Create Fan Page		
Market Fan Page		
Custom Fan Pages		
Invite Friends to Fan Page		
Advertising on Facebook		
Utilize LinkedIn®		
Create Account		
Connect to Colleagues and Classmates		
Post Business Updates		

Advertise		
Utilize Twitter®		
Create Account		
Follow People		
Tweet		
Automate		
Utilize YouTube®		
Create Account		
Create Content		
Post And Include Link		
Blog, Blog, Blog		
Internal Site		
External Site		
Comment		
Identify Related Blogs And Forums		
Contribute Quality Content		
Use URL For Signature		
Apply Google +1		

Create G-Mail Profile		
Install 1+ On Your Website		
Network For Likes		
Perform Social Bookmarking		
Digg®		
StumbleUpon®		
Reddit®		
Delicious®		

Networking Phase Description

Networking has become the newest and largest addition to the SEO landscape. Social and Business networking on the internet has transformed how businesses and people view the internet. The impacts of Facebook® and Twitter® alone have completely changed the world of media and the definition of community, and they have blurred the lines between personal and business relationships. This has created a huge opportunity for online businesses to reach customers in a very different way.

As with most things internet-related, ethical and unethical practices are abound. We promote the use of networking as a way to ethically market our business. Networking utilizes our business and personal relationships in ways that have value to both them and us.

Create a Plan

Social networking can be an overwhelming arena to enter. Every day there is a new idea, website, widget, app, etc. that can change how we interact with people. From the time I finish writing this to the time it is published, there could be dozens, if not hundreds, of new players in the business and social networking arena.

The best thing to do is to make a plan and stay focused. After you read this chapter, decide which tools or services you are going to make use of, and proceed methodically through the checklist. You may choose to only blog initially, so set a time period that each week you will focus on that and then review your results. Once you have completed that step, see if you want to add another tool or technique. It is easy to get overwhelmed if you wake up every day and say, "Okay, today I am going to tweet, blog, find friends, comment, update my website..." Be focused, or you will fail! Do not be a jack-of-all trades and master of none. Decide which ones will complement your strengths and focus on those at first.

Utilize Facebook®

We do not need to elaborate on the power of Facebook®. This phenomenon has changed the face of the internet and e-commerce. What once began as a way for college kids to get to know each other has become a commercial powerhouse. Currently, Facebook is the #1 website being accessed daily – WOW!

If you currently use Facebook, using it for business is a relatively simple next step. The way to make the transition from a personal networking tool to a business networking tool is to create a business page, or Fan page as it is called. In order to create a Fan page, you must have a personal account first.

Create a Fan Page

Go to facebook.com to sign in or create an account. Once you have a personal page, go to facebook.com/pages, then click on the button that says +Create Page. Select business type, then category, and enter what you want your page name to be. (You may have already reserved this name earlier when you registered your domain name.) At this point, it is similar to creating your personal page. Enter a photo or logo, invite friends, and enter information about your company. I would suggest that you skip inviting fans until you have finished creating the Fan page.

Market Fan Page

At this point, Facebook spoon-feeds you all of their great, organic (no cost), marketing techniques to get people to see your page. There are menu-driven prompts to help you:

- Invite Friends

- Import Contacts

- Post Updates On Your Wall

- Promote Site On Your Webpage

- Promote Site Via Advertising

Each one of these tools will increase traffic to your Fan page which will, in turn, increase traffic to your website. As you did with your website, you need to create a Call to Action on your Fan Page. Create a survey or have discounts specifically for Facebook users. Once they are on your page, you will want to ultimately direct them to your web site.

✪ **Important:** When you create the Fan Page, you will have a generic URL which looks something like this: www.facebook .com/pages/PlymouthFlowerStore/204568439603602. After you get 25 Fans to "Like" your site, then you can go to Edit Info on your Fan Page and you are allowed to select the original setup name as your URL so it now reads just www.facebook .com/pages/PlymouthFlowerStore/.

This is a unique feature of Facebook to motivate you to increase your number of Fans. This should be the first goal of your net-working plan. Inform your immediate friends first about the Fan Page. Once you have access to the new URL, you can use that one for a broader Facebook networking strategy.

✦ **Warning:** Do not over market to your Friends on your personal page. It is important to market to them initially to get them to join your fan page. Once they are Fans, you can market to them from your Fan page, but if you market to them too often, you will find yourself "unsubscribed or removed."

Custom Fan Pages

Facebook also allows developers to customize the Fan page to make it look more like a traditional website.

See one of Pam's businesses using the standard Facebook Template: www.facebook.com/pmcustomweddings/

Now see it on a Pam's custom Fan Page:

That is not to say that the standard template is not worthwhile. People are very comfortable with the look and feel of Facebook, but the more you can do to impress visitors and keep them coming back, the better.

Advertising on Facebook

This is the first time we discuss any type of paid advertising as part of your internet marketing strategy. We postponed discussing this specifically because we do not want you to focus on it until you have implemented effective SEO practices. Why? Because advertising works! You will increase traffic significantly once you advertise, but if you do not have a well-optimized web site, marketing approach, and conversion strategy, all that traffic will be wasted.

Facebook advertising is a good way to test the advertising waters. It has a very friendly tool to create and submit ads. When you are logged into Facebook and on your Fan page, you will see "place an ad" in right column. Once you click on that, you will have an entry screen. At this point you can choose whether to point customers to your website or your Fan page. You can then either create an ad in the form or upload an ad image that you created.

The next step is to target your ad. Your targeting options are:

- Location
- Age
- Birthdate
- Gender
- Interests
- Type of connections
- Relationships
- Languages
- Education
- Company

Select an option for each one of these categories to identify your target market. Depending on which options you select will determine how many people you will reach with your advertisement.

The final step is to select your budget. At this point you need to understand Pay per Click (PPC). Most internet advertising is charged when a potential customer clicks on your ad. This is called PPC. You can set a daily budget or a total budget. Facebook will tell you the average Cost per Click (CPC) so that you can determine how many potential customers may visit as a result of your budget. The CPC can be customized if you do not want to pay the maximum. Put in your billing information and you are off to the races!

○ **Important:** If you follow our best practices, advertising will work for you. You will most likely use the entire budget that you enter. Only enter the budget amount that you are willing to spend.

Utilize LinkedIn®

LinkedIn is a professional networking tool. It is very different from Facebook because it does not revolve around your personal life. It is basically a huge resume database where people connect based on their professional relationship with you. That is not to say that sometimes personal lines do not get crossed, as with Facebook, but the intent of LinkedIn is for business reasons. This makes it a much easier tool to use to promote your business because that is what visitors expect.

Create LinkedIn Account

You create an account on LinkedIn based upon your personal name. Once your account is created, you create a Profile similar to what you would include on your resume. This is actually one of the key uses of LinkedIn. Recruiters will often search LinkedIn to find experienced people they can recruit directly.

Connect to Colleagues and Classmates

LinkedIn uses the term *Connect* to define how to add people to your network. Once you have created your profile, LinkedIn will provide you with "People You May Know" based upon your previous jobs and college education. This makes it easy. Do not hesitate to Connect to anyone you have worked with or went to school with. This tool seldom exposes you or them to any information you are not comfortable seeing unlike social networking sites.

Post Business Updates

Everyone's home page on LinkedIn has a wall like Facebook called Updates. Updates include entries from both you and your connections. This is where you would post something such as a new product or an event you are holding. You can also provide a link to a blog, article, etc. If you "Like" something you have seen on someone else's update, it shows up to all of your connections. Your goal is for people to "Like" your post so that your connections will be sharing to their connections. At this moment, I have the following view from my LinkedIn Network statistics:

Your Connections Your trusted friends and colleagues	205
Two degrees away Friends of friends; each connected to one of your connections	30,700+
Three degrees away Reach these users through a friend and one of their friends	2,496,200+
Total users you can contact through an Introduction	2,527,200+

As you can see, this can be a powerful tool to reach a significant number of people.

Everything I described above is part of the free subscription. If you want to email your network or get introductions, you can get that as part of your paid subscriber package.

Join Groups

Other ways to network within LinkedIn is to join industry or company-related groups. These groups operate like discussion forums or blogs where you can provide targeted industry specific content, and it is another place that it is acceptable to promote your products or services.

Advertise

Yes, LinkedIn, like everyone else, has realized that the real money is in advertising, not subscribers. To get started, go to http://www.linkedin.com/advertising, click on Get Started, and enter the basic information, URL, logo, etc. On the next page you will enter the ad, which should point to a landing page on your website. Next, you will select the options to identify your target audience based upon:

- Geography

- Company

- Job Title

- Group

- Gender

- Age

LinkedIn will show you the number of people in its network that meet your criteria. On the next page, as with Facebook, you will enter CPC (Cost per Click) or you may enter CPM (Cost per Impressions), which is a relatively unique option. You will then create a daily budget.

Utilize Twitter®

Twitter is also a phenomenon – there is just no other word for it. It has changed how the public interacts with celebrities and other public figures. It has created a whole new language in sound bites and abbreviations, and it has changed how companies interact with their customers. Who would have thought how much news could be made out of 140 character messages?

Create Account

Again, create an account that uses your business name, logo, and website URL. This account should not be for personal use. Unless you are a recognized expert in your field or you are a celebrity, keep your business and personal tweets separate.

Follow People

The key to finding Followers is to follow other people. Search for people in the same industry as you and Follow them. This performs two purposes. The first is to see what type of information they are tweeting; the second is to see if they will in turn Follow you.

Tweet

As you obtain Followers, you should begin tweeting. The tweeting can simply be links to blogs you create, opinions about your industry, tips, and tricks. As your following grows, and you have established that you provide quality content, you can begin to promote your website, or business. If possible, include discounts or specials for Followers. Otherwise, they will learn to not click on your links.

Since, as we discussed earlier, you have to focus your networking plan, you will have to decide if tweeting 140 character words of wisdom is your strength or if it is a better tool for you if you use it as a way to publicize a blog, article, or press release.

Automate

Gaining Followers is the big challenge; it takes time and patience. Following people via an automated tool is an option to increase your Followers. This is one area where we recommend purchasing help. You can purchase a tool or service (see the Appendix for examples) that will target people or companies that you identify, and it will systematically follow their Followers. Twitter restricts how many people you can follow in a day, so you can schedule how many people you want to follow.

This process does not directly get you Followers. The individuals still have to choose to follow you, which is the intent and design of Twitter's model. Automating an ethical approach is both practical and ethical. Automating an unethical approach only makes it worse.

Utilize YouTube®

If your product or services are compatible with video, then YouTube may be the networking opportunity for you. Obviously, if you are a musician or performer, YouTube is the way to go. Videos are considered the number one way to retain visitors on your site. A short, less-than 30-second video has a higher chance of getting through to your potential customer than asking them to read 30 seconds worth of content.

Whereas we did not recommend placing many videos on your homepage, we do not have any problem with posting lots of videos on YouTube. An extra benefit of having a YouTube video is that you can include your URL in the description on the YouTube page, which then gives you a high-quality backlink.

Create Account

Use the Gmail® account that you created earlier to log in to YouTube. Again, make sure to separate business from personal. Visitors do not want to see video of your cat chasing your dog...(or maybe they do). Once you have logged in, go to the upper right hand corner of the page to the drop down menu next to your Gmail address, select Settings, then Profile Settings. Complete the profile page.

✪ **Important:** To create your profile name, use your company name or domain name. This will allow your URL to look like www.youtube.com/plymouthflowerstore.

Create Content

We are not video experts, so you should go elsewhere to get advice on creating high-quality video. However, we can provide you with the SEO considerations when uploading video content to YouTube. When you upload videos, you have the option to complete the following information.

- File name: Do not upload "video1-9-2012", use a keyword related name such as "Creating_A_Bouquet"

- Title: Do not waste this critical real estate. Make sure it is keyword driven as well. "Creating the Perfect Holiday Bouquet - Tutorial." YouTube only uses the first 66 characters in its search results so make sure the interesting part of the title is first.

- Description: Include quality keyword-driven content that hooks a customer into watching the video. In addition, always include your URL in the description.

- Tags: keywords, keywords, keywords

Advertise

YouTube has a very robust advertising program. Depending on the target demographics (age and sex) for your product or service, this may be a great advertising medium. YouTube has a different demographic from the other sites we mentioned. Here are the demographics of their 300 million users! 71% of their users are under 49 – not the right target audience for denture cream.

Ages	Percentage of YouTube Users
2 – 18	18%
18–34	25%
35–49	27%
50+	29%
Sex	**Percentage of YouTube Users**
Male	53%
Female	47%

(Youtube.com Traffic and Demographic Statistics by Quantcast)[iv]

You can advertise on the pages with text or graphics, or if you want to go all out, you can create video ads that will be played at the beginning of high-traffic videos. Go to http://www.youtube.com/t /advertising overview for more information.

Blog, Blog, Blog

Recently, I was doing some keyword research for a client, and I noticed that there were over 3.5 million searches that month on Google that referenced "learn how to blog"... I wish they just asked me. Blogging is easy; just start typing. How much to blog? What to blog? Where to blog? Those are the more difficult questions to answer.

Blogging is writing. If you do not like to write, then focus your efforts on one of the other networking options. As you have seen, there are options for everyone's talents. It is better not to blog than it is to be a poor blogger. I heard a statistic recently that there are currently more bloggers than readers. That puts it in perspective, doesn't it?

Blogging has the following three basic purposes:

- Creates fresh quality content that is related to your products or services to increase your SEO through keyword utilization and quality links to your site.

- Establishes you and your company as an expert in your industry to lend credibility to the products or services you offer.

- Creates followers that are interested in your content so that you have a captive audience to market your products, services or advertisements.

So the answer to "What to blog?" is, "Anything that serves one or more of these purposes noted above." How often? Our favorite answer... "It depends." It depends on the length of the content, your availability, the number of followers, etc. If you have short content and a significant number of followers, you should blog daily. It will keep your traffic coming, and it could support advertising revenue and marketing strategy. If your content is complex or you do not have many views or followers yet, do not overdo it. Focus on quality content that will attract followers first.

Internal Site

Most hosting companies provide tools that enable you to include a blog as part of your website. WordPress is a blogger platform first and foremost. If you have this technology, it is beneficial to blog on your own site. You do not have to blog on your site, but it does help the SEO of your site by creating lots of quality content and can attract traffic directly to your site. If you blog on an internal site, then use Twitter to attract people to your blog.

External Site

Blogging on an external site, such as Google's blogger.com, gives you a different benefit. Once you build your content and your followers, Google's quality rating of backlinks will be high. It will have its own PageRank, and it will serve as another landing page for your website.

You may find that there are industry-specific blogs that will suit your purpose. Pam has both. Her internal ones are kept very clean with less frequent, high-quality content. She uses her external site to pilot different marketing strategies; it is where she allows advertisements and other external links.

There is no definite right or wrong answer to where your blogs should be or how many blogs you should create. The real answer is, again, "It depends." A successful marketing plan will evolve as new information becomes available. If you find that the external blog you created is attracting 200 visitors to your site, try creating a different blog and see if you can double your visitors.

Comment

Commenting is like mini-blogging. You provide comments on other people's blogs. The value of commenting is that you are embedding links to your website as part of your signature or subscriber information. Another value is that you are creating opportunities to impress people enough to come to your site. Commenting is pretty straightforward, but there are a few points to consider. They are described below.

Identify Related Blogs and Forums

We do not advocate posting on unrelated forums just to get a backlink. This is called trolling. It sets a precedent for unethical SEO activities that could impact search engine rankings or impact your site's credibility with visitors. If you search, there are plenty of sites that are related to your industry or your interests. Find these and establish your credibility through thoughtful, quality content.

Most quality sites will not allow you to post product links in your comment or allow you to self-promote. Conversely, you have to decide if you will allow comments on your blogs. You can also choose to review comments before posting them so that you can prevent *trolls* or product links in your blog.

Contribute Quality Content

So, what is quality content?

Let's assume you found a Blog that focused on new and innovative flower arrangements. You could read a blog you liked and comment as follows:

> "Great post, I liked what you had to say," signed www.plymouthflowerstore.com"

> or

> "Your post reminds me about our current 2 for 1 sale, click here."

Stop! That is not quality commenting. Consider comments that are more engaging in order to get your comment posted and have the possibility of a quality backlink:

> "Thanks for the information. One thing I like to do when I buy a bouquet is to put a single flower in each of my bathrooms. It makes me feel like I get more for my money," Pam from www.plymouthflowerstore.com.

Use URL in Signature

For most blogs, you must complete a registration form in order to submit a comment. On the registration form, you will be asked for your URL. This allows your signature to show your name, and it will also be a hyperlink to your website. You should be able to see from other people's comments if the blog owner will allow links or signatures to be embedded in the text.

Adopt Google +1®

Google entered the social networking market with the introduction of Google +1 in 2011. The intent of +1 is to combine the use of "like" with its search results. As you click +1 for a website, it will get stored in your profile, and if you allow it, Google will let anyone else in your "Circle" see your rating. A Circle is Google's term for Friends or Connections. Another impact of +1 is that once you +1 a site, that site will always show up in the top or your search results for that category or keywords. I do not know the algorithm that determines when it does and does not show up, but it only happens when you are logged in to Google. At this point, Google +1 has not been adopted by everyone, but it is only a matter of time.

Create G-mail Profile

You most likely already have an account for your website. You may want to create a separate account for your +1 profile. Create a profile based upon your professional interests, not personal ones. Again, keep business and personal networking accounts separate. As of this printing of the SEO Manifesto, Google did not have a business profile option, only personal, so you will have to use your personal profile format in order to link it to your site. Google is working on creating a business profile, so keep checking back.

Install 1+ on your website

Login to http://www.google.com/webmasters/+1/button/ to get access to the HTML for the Google +1 button. Copy the code snippet for the +1 button and install the button on your home page. It is best to put it somewhere near the top of your page in order for visitors to readily see it and click on it.

Network for Likes

As with the rest of your networking activities, this requires that you reach out and create an online community. In this case, it is the Google Circle. As you create this community, you will want to market your products to them so that they "Like" you. Also, as you tweet or blog, you can direct them to your site to click on Like, even if they are not in your circle. It may not be obvious to everyone, but we are fairly sure that the number of Likes that you accumulate over the next few years is going to become a key component to Google's algorithm and ranking criteria.

Perform Social Bookmarking

Social bookmarking sites use your interests to help you "bookmark" or organize websites. There are several sites that offer this service, and they each have a different approach on how they accomplish this. Ebizma.com ranks the four most popular social bookmarking sites (after Twitter) as the following:

Digg®

Digg presents articles ranging from celebrity gossip to product reviews. The homepage displays the most recent submission as the default view. This allows anyone to get some short-term high-traffic exposure. With Digg, you submit a link and a description, so if the description is engaging, you are more likely to get some traffic to your site.

To create an account at www.digg.com, use your company or domain name as your username. Once you are a member, it is very easy to use the tool. It allows you to enter a link, update the title and description, and provide a high-level category. Once you create the link, it will be posted with an opportunity to comment.

People will come across your content several ways. Over time, you will hopefully attract Followers. When you post, it will show up on the homepage of your Followers under "My News." You can also be "Dugg" if someone searches on a keyword and comes across your post. Lastly--and this is when you know you have hit the jackpot with your post--you show up on the "Trending" view which shows the current highest viewed posts.

In addition, Digg allows you to put widgets on your website for visitors to "Digg" your content directly as you create it. Go to http://about.digg.com/publishers to see the latest technical updates for people who are creating content.

StumbleUpon®

StumbleUpon is a member-only site. Go to www.Stumble-Upon.com and create an account with your company or domain name. StumbleUpon will ask if it can confirm your account with your Facebook account. Do not do it for your business Stumble-Upon account. It will automatically update your personal profile in Facebook with all of your bookmarking activity which will flood your Friends walls. For reasons mentioned previously, we recommend keeping Facebook a more personal focus.

StumbleUpon's approach is to combine your profile information and interests in order to present you with focused, personalized search results. Sound a little like Big Brother? Well, that's because it is. The goal is to get you to sites that are of most interest to you, without having to search through pages and pages of results. In addition to this customization, a site must be high-ranked in order to be listed. This is the opposite of the neutrality assumed by typical search engines, and it works more like a shopping site based upon reviews and pricing.

So, can you see where this is headed? The person with the best networking skills gets to the top of this list. You can control the search results outcome much easier than with a search engine, though "easier" does not mean "easy." You will have to create great articles, catchy titles, and descriptions that hook the reader to "Like" you. Uploaded or linked videos work great for a bookmarking site like StumbleUpon.

Reddit®

Reddit is similar to Digg. Reddit's home page defaults to "What's Hot," so links that are generating the most traffic in that moment get the high ranking. You do not need to be a member to view Reddit, but you need an account to submit links.

Go to www.reddit.com and create an account with your company or domain name. On the main page, you can submit a link to your blog, website, article, etc. Reddit is also similar to Digg in that the user community, not your interests, dictates what is showing up in the lists. However, Reddit offers several categories across the top of each page to provide organization of the popular posts. Commenting and voting are what gets you at the top of the list on Reddit. Also, their site is organized by "subreddits" which have different communities based upon certain categories. Depending on your product or service, you target your links to specific sub-reddits to attract some interest.

Reddit, as an in-person community, is growing as well. Users are using tools like Meetup.com to set-up events to socialize. These "Meetups" revolve around their specific interests. We will not cover Meetups.com further in this guide, but we would suggest you look into it if you have a product or service that would benefit from your seeing people in person. Plymouth's Flower Store could use Meetups.com to organize a charity event, cocktail party, etc.

Delicious®

"The tastiest bookmarks on the web" is their tagline. I love this URL. It is easy to remember, and the domain name shows up in a significant number of other searches unrelated to social book-marking.

Create an account at www.delicious.com. Once you create it, it asks you to add buttons to your toolbar. Delicious is unique because it also imports your current bookmarks to the Delicious site so that you have all your bookmarks in one place. Your book-marks can either be made private or public. If you are posting it publically, such as your blog, you can add a title, tags, and description.

Similar to Twitter, you can add people to your network whose bookmarks you want to follow. Delicious focuses more on their Hotlist and Fresh bookmarks, presenting the most popular links regardless of category.

Conclusion

This chapter needs a conclusion! If you feel overwhelmed after reading this chapter, don't fret. Networking is currently the most complex and dynamic component of SEO. A new player can enter this space any minute and change the game completely. You can spend all your effort in one area, only to find that you did not have any impact. Performing the same activity on another networking activity can yield great results.

As I mentioned at the beginning of this chapter, align your product or services with your networking strength and then focus. I recommend you begin by selecting one networking site from each of the following categories based upon your product or service and target audience:

- Facebook or LinkedIn or YouTube

- Blogging or Tweeting or Commenting

- Digg or StumbleUpon or Reddit or Delicious

Start with this approach and see how your traffic changes. If you do not get any additional traffic after three months of an approach, move on to another approach. If you are getting a good response, keep with it and, eventually, you can add a similar site. The key to networking is finding an approach that you enjoy and are comfortable with.

If you do not have an interest in any of these activities in this chapter, you need to rethink your business model. You may need to hire people to perform these activities, or you may need to spend more time and money on traditional marketing.

Remember, the value of all of these activities in this chapter is that they lead to organic growth where the only cost is your time, not your checkbook. If you have more money than time, you can adopt a different strategy. Bottom line: there are no shortcuts. It is either going to cost you time or money.

Chapter 7: Advertise

Advertising Phase Checklist

The following table lists the steps necessary to complete the Advertising phase of your website. Use this checklist to track your progress in this phase. The section that follows includes descriptions of each of the steps listed below.

Steps	Target Date	Completed Date
Create Plan and Approach		
Create Conversion Approach		
Establish Landing Pages		
Test And Validate		
Organic Online Advertising		
Create and Submit Press Releases		
Create And Submit Articles		
Paid Advertising		
Establish Budget		
Determine Approach		

Select Providers		
Write Ads		
Post Ads		

Advertising Phase Description

You are probably asking yourself, "Wasn't the last chapter about advertising?" Actually, networking is considered marketing, and advertising is a component of marketing as well. They are both part of your marketing strategy. Traditionally, advertising has involved paying someone else to get your message out to the market. That is still the case with internet-advertising, but we also categorize press releases and articles as part of the advertising phase. When you are social networking, you may be less willing to promote your product or service directly so that you do not alienate your Friends.

In the Advertising Phase, we will focus on activities that are specifically intended to promote your product or service. Advertising is a unique part of your overall marketing strategy because it has the potential to be extremely costly. At the same time, it has the ability to rapidly increase traffic to your site. SEO focuses on organic increases in traffic, and advertising generally focuses on buying the most traffic for the dollar.

Create Conversion Approach

Before you begin advertising, you need to create a conversion approach. A conversion happens when a person goes from being a visitor to a customer, either by making a purchase or performing a specific action such as clicking on an advertisement. Your conversion approach has to be created to support and align with your advertising approach. For example, your blog posts may increase traffic to your site and increase your SEO. Your advertising strategy should be created to drive conversions, such as a sale.

Establish Landing Pages

One of the most important conversion approaches is the creation of landing pages. A landing page is the first page a visitor sees when clicking on an ad or a link from an external site. Many people try to optimize their homepage as the landing page for all visitors, but this forces them to look more deeply into your site to find what they are looking for.

For example, let's say PlymouthFlowerStore.com runs an ad for Valentine's Day. An effective strategy is to have the visitor click on the ad and land on the page that allows them to order specific flowers for that holiday. A less-effective strategy is to have them land on the homepage that shows all occasions. The visitor would then have to click on another link to get to the Valentine's Day page. If this happens, you can be sure that you will lose some potential customers. The term for losing visitors after one page is called your *bounce rate* and if you lose them prior to a conversion that is your *abandonment rate.*

All traditional sales-related industries realize that they have to focus on selling a customer in the moment. In grocery stores, companies pay a premium to be on an aisle endcap or at eye level on the shelves. For car sales, the close rate on customers buying the first time they walk into the showroom is significantly higher than if you let them leave to think about it. Many of us are emotional buyers with short attention spans, so your landing page strategy is to take full advantage of the opportunity while the customer is on your site.

Landing pages have to be simple and relate exactly to your ad. If you have five ads running, then you might need five different landing pages. These landing pages may not have any internal links that point to it, so do not worry about having to modify your homepage menu or navigation. The landing page should be linked to the rest or your site so that visitors can view other products and services that you have to offer.

✪ **Important:** Make sure the Call to Action is on the landing page or no more than one click away.

Test and Validate

One of the best ways to ensure you have an effective conversion approach is to test and validate it. We recommend that you create parallel ad campaigns with separate landing pages. You would then run separate ads simultaneously for a period of time. It can be as short as a day or as long as a month. At the end of the time period you can compare the effectiveness of each.

The beauty of online advertising is the ability to quickly test and modify approaches as more information and data are reviewed. Do not make this a one-time event either. Do this continually until you are completely satisfied with your conversions.

The conversion rate is the measure of the effectiveness of your conversion approach. It is the percentage of visitors who performed your desired action such as a purchase. This is a simple calculation of the number of customers divided by the number of visitors. For example, if for every 1000 visitors to your landing page yields 100 sales, you have 10% conversion rate. I know what your next question is going to be, "What should my conversion rate be?" Well, you already know this answer, "It depends." It depends upon the product, the service, the time of year, the economy, etc.

The most important metric is ultimately the number of sales and associated revenue. If your conversion rate is only 1%, but you are meeting your revenue projections, you do not have to focus on only conversion rate. You may only have to focus on increasing traffic. If your conversion rate is high, but your revenues are low, you need to evaluate your product pricing and try increasing it. Or, you may want to work on additional SEO and marketing strategies to increase traffic.

When you test and validate, you can also test different price points for your product. You may not be able to test different price points at the same time, but you could try one price for a week and then switch it up. Or, you could target one ad with a coupon and another without. As you can see, the options are virtually limitless.

Organic Advertising

Create and Submit Press Releases

Press releases can be part of both an organic and paid approach. In the following section we will discuss the organic approach. The approach for submitting an internet press release is the same as it was prior to the use of the internet for this purpose. The format is identical as well. A press release is an opportunity to advertise a significant event within your company such as the launch of your website or the creation of a new product or service. The purpose is not to offer a discount or promotion. You will not get picked up by your local newspaper if you use a press release to offer a 10% holiday special. There are several companies that use them in this way, but we believe that borders on the unethical.

A typical press release has the following components:

Title: Short and interesting

Summary: Use keywords and make it compelling so that people want to read further.

Body: This is the story. Make it appealing and have enough--but not too much-- information about your business. You want to create enough interest so that the reader will want to visit your site to find out more.

Tags: Keywords

Industry, Address, Contact Info: This information is actually the most critical. News services will have feeds from each of the major press release companies that are sorted by industry or location. Your local newspaper will have feed that pulls in any press release that have your town in the article. This is a traditional and effective way of getting free advertising. Many newspapers will either publish this content in their print media or on their associated web site. Remember, this is the business that they are in, so if you can make your press release truly newsworthy, then you will get picked up.

If you are targeting your press release for your local area, focus on a "hook" that will generate interest by the local newspaper. For example:

Poor Summary:

Plymouth's Flower Store on Main Street in Plymouth now allows you to order flowers from their website.

Good Summary

Plymouth businesswoman sees tremendous growth opportunity by launching PlymouthFlowerStore.com.

Would that second summary make you want to read the rest of the press release? The people reviewing the press releases are local people like you. If they find themselves reading the body of the press release, then you have a great chance of getting published.

While there is not a charge for a newspaper to publish a press release, the press release websites will charge to have you posted on their site, and to "help you" get your press releases published in more places. We have not found a significant difference between free versus paid press release services. You may have to pay if you want to use this as a primary marketing strategy. Most "free" sites will limit how many press releases you can post without upgrading to a paid subscription.

(To see sites that offer free or paid press releases, go to the Appendix.)

Create and Submit Articles

Articles are basically a combination of a press release and a blog. In an article, you are writing something similar to a blog, but you are not posting it on your own site or blog. As with a press release, you are submitting it to be published and it can be re-published or circulated by anyone. It is valuable because many of the article sites have high search engine rankings of their own, and the articles can serve as high-ranked backlinks for your website.

Articles can be as simple as a text-based article, or they can be as complex as a fully customized mini website, depending on the site where you post the article. As with almost every other marketing activity we have discussed, the more people who read your article and "Like" it, or rate it with a high score, the more visibility you will get on their website.

There are several article sites listed in the Appendix. These sites generally present articles in one of the following types of formats.

Ezines

Ezines focus on categorizing articles into newsletters. Once you create an article, it is categorized and captured along with other related articles to be read or distributed as a newsletter. These newsletters are then presented to subscribers both on the website and via e-mail. Any publisher or individual can then use your article (only in its entirety) on their website. The advantage of this is that you get a backlink from their site; the disadvantage is that they get the SEO keyword value of your content on their site.

As with press releases, frequent article writers will have to upgrade to a paid membership. In order to find the right Ezine for you, simply search for "<my industry> ezines." For example, when we search for "florist ezines," Google returns several articles that people have written in Ezines. You can review these articles, and, if they are receiving votes, decide if that might be an Ezine that has some potential for you.

Mini Websites

Mini Websites have become one of the newest, most popular ways to promote websites. There are several article directories that host these mini websites instead of traditional text-based articles. Squidoo.com, an article site, coined the term *lens* for its mini websites. If you go to this site, you will notice that its home page is much different. Instead of showing links to articles, it shows a picture or graphic.

The process of submitting an article is similar to that of an E-zine, but with lens pages or mini websites, you publish it to a template that includes your graphics, logo, advertising, etc. In addition, since visuals are so much more important in this format, the "hook" is not the text or title, but the image. To build one yourself requires the same willingness and aptitude as you would need to create a WordPress site. If you want help, most website designers now specialize in these "one-page sites" as well.

Paid Advertising

The number of ways to pay for advertising is more numerous than ever with the emergence of internet advertising. You may opt for traditional paid advertising, such as in print, television, or radio. However, if you are going after a specific target market and are offering a product service that can be purchased online, focus most, if not all, of your advertising budget on internet advertising. If you have deep pockets, it could mean that you are paying people to read this book for you. But, seriously, if you have the money and are not looking for an immediate return on investment, you can spread it around. However, if you are like most new businesses on the internet, you are being sensible with your advertising dollars.

All of the organic marketing and SEO strategies we have discussed will bring traffic to your site. So why pay for advertising?

To grow your business quickly:

Using effective organic SEO and internet marketing techniques can start bringing traffic to your site and can show gradual progress on a monthly basis. Using paid advertising can show the same growth on a daily or even hourly basis.

To Perform a Proof of Concept:

Are you confident that your product or service will sell online? Are you willing to invest six months of time increasing your traffic, only to find that your sales assumptions were incorrect? Paid advertising will bring traffic to your site quickly so you can test your business model. Are people performing the Call to Action? Are people staying on my site? Am I getting return visitors? Even if you have a successful business model, in a proof of concept, you may actually spend more in advertising than you make. However, the data you receive in return will be worth every penny. You will learn about your bounce rate, your conversion rate, etc.

To Reach a Critical Mass:

You may offer a product or service that is only profitable if you have a high volume. For example, companies like Zappos.com only became profitable after they achieved sales in the hundreds of thousands. Their business model required that they stock shoes in their own warehouses, whereas many other products are drop shipped (delivered direct from the manufacturer). Zappos was not making a profit on a single pair of shoes, because they may have had to purchase in volume from the manufacturer. It was not until they reached a critical mass of thousands of shoe sales that they actually could turn a profit.

Establish Budget

If your business model or growth strategy requires paid advertising, the first place you start is with a budget. As we discussed in Chapter 2, you should already have an idea of your financial model and expected ROI for your business. Based upon this model, you should have an idea of what you are willing to spend on advertising.

The good news with internet advertising is that, in most cases, you can modify your advertising budget daily, hourly, or even in real time. Another benefit is that advertising on the internet can become a variable cost as opposed to a fixed cost. That means that you can tie your advertising budget directly to your revenue. There are several different approaches for paid internet advertising. Here are the most common approaches:

Pay per Click (PPC)

PPC or Cost per Click (CPC) is the most common approach. In this approach, your ad is on someone else's site, and every time someone clicks on it you pay that site a fee.

Pay per Impression (CPM)

CPM or Cost per thousand (the M represent the roman numeral for 1000) is rapidly gaining popularity. CPM is the equivalent of billboard advertising of the internet. With CPM, you pay to have the ad show up regardless of whether it is clicked on. This is often billed as a cost per 1000 views.

Pay per Action (PPA)

PPA is an approach in which you pay only when a specific action occurs, such as a purchase. In this case, you typically have *affiliates* that help you to sell your product, and you pay the affiliate if someone they refer makes a purchase. In order to have an affiliate relationship with someone, you need a way to track where each sale originates. We have listed some affiliate brokers in the Appendix that can perform this tracking for you.

With any of these approaches, you need to determine your advertising cost per sale (CPS). With Pay per Action, it is easy. You know you will only pay if you sell, so you can give up a percentage of your revenue to the affiliate. With Pay per Click and Pay per Impression you have to initially guess. (Yes, you read this correctly.) You will have to guess until you can analyze your business and establish some sales metrics or measurements. An example of some sales metrics follows:

(This is going to be a math word problem, so I apologize if I bring back any painful grade school memories.)

> Pam sells ribbons online which are drop-shipped from the manufacturer. For every sale she has a gross profit of $5.00. In the first month, she chooses to use paid advertising on a search engine with a CPC of 50 cents. Her assumption or "guess" was that one out of five visitors would buy ribbons. This gives her a 20% expected *conversion rate*. This means she was guessing her CPS to be $2.50 (5 people x 50 cents) for every $5.00 of sales, giving her a profit of $2.50 per sale.
>
> At the end of month 1, Pam had 1000 visitors from paid advertising, which equals 1000 clicks, which cost her $500.00, but she only had a conversion rate of 10% which means only 1 in 10 people bought ribbons. So, she ended up with 100 people buying ribbons, which generated $500 in revenues which gave her a CPS of $5.00. As you can see, this will not work because she guessed incorrectly. Her advertising costs equaled her revenues, so her profit was zero.

Is this good news or bad news? Well, it depends. Pam now has the metrics to make a more informed decision and no longer has to guess. The good news is that her ribbons have a market; the bad news is that her advertising strategy did not match her financial expectations.

These metrics, which we will talk about in more length in the next chapter, will help her to redefine her advertising strategy. She now has data that she can apply to her advertising strategy. Her options are to develop strategies to increase her conversion rate, change her pricing model or reduce her CPC, and possibly find a cheaper advertising platform. Or, she may suspend the paid advertising strategy and just work on her organic approach for a few months.

Select Providers

Once you have an idea of your budget and what type of advertising approach you want, you have to decide on which advertising provider to spend it. Your options are all the places on the internet that have significant traffic, including search engines, networking sites, blogs, etc. We reviewed in Chapter 6 how to advertise on Facebook and LinkedIn. You can also advertise on the social bookmarking sites, article sites, YouTube, etc.

Google AdWords® is the 800 pound gorilla in this market. AdWords has 65% of the search engine traffic and 85% of the advertising revenues. When you advertise with AdWords, not only are you buying ad space on their search engine, you are buying ad space on thousands of sites in the Google Network from people who have signed up for their AdSense® product. AdSense is the product, which allows anyone to show Google Ads on their site.

Most of these providers have similar prices and approaches. You can go with one option, or you can go with many. We would not recommend that you overdue it. Try different approaches and different providers for as short as a day. You will be able to determine immediately if you are getting increased traffic from your ads.

Write Ads

Writing a two-line internet ad is harder than it sounds. The fewer the words, the more important it is to be clear and concise. Unfortunately, we all cannot use "Got Milk?" or "The Computer for the Rest of Us." Those short slogans cost millions of dollars to develop and package. What we can do is take advantage of the small piece of real estate in an internet ad by adopting the following strategies.

Use Keywords: The search engines match the content of the search to the keywords in your ad. Make sure you have your important keywords in the title.

Be Focused: If you own a flower store, your ad should be about a specific arrangement or holiday. You can create a separate ad for each situation. Do not create ads that are general.

Let's take a look at a building supply store. Nobody is searching on the internet for "building supplies." They are search for a particular product like kitchen cabinets. Offer a single product as the hook for your ad.

Use Promotions: Even if you are paying for advertising, you will still be competing with other advertisers on the page. Differentiate yourself through special offers and promotions.

Let us assume Plymouth's Flower Store is using Google AdWords for its paid advertising campaign. It has created a campaign to target only the towns in its immediate vicinity.

Ineffective Ad:

Order Flowers Online

Every Flower Imaginable

Great Prices

www.PlymouthFlowerStore.com

Effective Ad:

Mother's Day Bouquets

Save 20% with our online coupon!

This Week Only

www.PlymouthFlowerStore.com

Spend some time creating these ads. Review some of the tremendous number of resources on the internet for writing ads. Check out what ads your competitors are running. In addition to text ads, most providers allow you to post graphic ads. They usually give you three or four different size options. Designing a small and effective graphic ad is even more challenging. You may want to hire some help for this activity. If you go to one of the freelance designer sites in the Appendix, you will find resources that could easily create these types of ads for as little as $100.00 per ad.

Post Ads

Advertising providers have many different options when you are ready to post an ad. Some of the options include:

- Start and Finish Date

- Daily, Weekly, Monthly, or Maximum budget

- Time of day

- Location: country, state, town

- Language

- Demographics: Age, Gender

- Interests, Clubs, Background, etc.

The flexibility of online ads is tremendous. Stick with providers that offer this type of targeted advertising. That way it ensures that your ads are getting to the right people and that you are getting the most value for your ad.

So, the final step of posting your ad is straightforward, but it does require attention to detail. Make sure you set a maximum budget, regardless of your CPC. Until you understand your conversion rate, you need to set a maximum budget that you can afford, even if you do not make a single sale.

Most online ad companies require a credit card for payment, so you will be billed immediately. Review your ads frequently once you post so that you can make adjustments while you learn your market.

Chapter 8: Track

Tracking Phase Checklist

The following table lists the steps necessary to complete the Tracking Phase of the project. Once you start tracking, you continue for the life of your business, which is why we greyed out the Completed Date below for some of the activities. Use this checklist to track your progress in this phase. The section that follows includes descriptions of each of the steps listed below.

Steps	Target Date	Completed Date
Capture Analytics		
Select Provider		
Utilize Monthly Tracking Spreadsheet		
Analyze and Act		
Organic Tracking		
Total Visits		
Search Engines		
Direct Traffic		
Referrals		
Bounce Rate		

Actions		
Conversion Rate		
Google PageRank		
Backlinks		
Search Engine Results Position		
Advertising Tracking		
Impressions		
Clicks		
Click Through Rate		
Validate Cost and ROI		

Tracking Phase Description

The Tracking Phase can be the most intimidating phase if you are not a numbers person. This phase begins almost immediately after you launch your website and continues until you close down your business. It includes the ongoing review of different measurements, which are typically called metrics, but is also referred to by Google as analytics. The terms "metrics" and "analytics" can be used interchangeably.

Capture Analytics

There are several different tools that can help you capture the analytic information. Every search engine provides them free of charge and they can be purchased from several 3rd party providers. Most of the metrics you review will be obtained by putting a code snippet on your web pages. A snippet is just techie term for a short piece of code. This snippet will allow your analytics provider to measure traffic on your site.

Select Provider

As you could probably guess, Google is the number one analytics tool used by small businesses. It is an online tool that is very robust and integrates well with the other Google products like AdWords and AdSense®.

Large businesses use commercial 3rd- party tools that are installed locally to track all of their internal and external traffic. Commercial tools are even more robust and provide a whole other level of flexibility, but they also are much more expensive and complex to manage.

We are not in the product review business, but, in certain cases, we do inform you of which tools we use. We use StatCounter at www.statcounter.com. (We do not receive any compensation from StatCounter.) Statcounter is free unless you upgrade to a premium account for very high-volume websites. It may not be as robust as Google Analytics, but that is why we like it. It is easy to use, and it has the metrics in which we are most interested-- right at our fingertips. All of the metrics which we are focusing on initially can be provided by almost any of the companies that offer this service. Also, both Pam and I periodically look at our metrics on all three search engines because there are most definitely some inconsistencies between them. It is interesting to see different perspectives.

Utilize Monthly SEO Tracking Spreadsheet

In order to capture the most important metrics, we suggest you use the Monthly SEO Tracking Spreadsheet that we have included in the Appendix. Remember, we have also included an electronic version of this spreadsheet at http://www.SeoManifesto.com/appendix.html.

Analytics providers give you so much data, you can easily get overwhelmed by information overload. We suggest you initially focus only on the most important key metrics that we have captured on the Tracking Spreadsheet. Once you are comfortable with the data on the Tracking Spreadsheet, you can expand it to include more. In addition, the activity of filling in the spreadsheet will be a more effective way to understand and interact with the data than by merely looking at the metrics on an analytics website.

Analyze and Act

Once you begin to capture your site analytics, you will have information that we hope will motivate you to act. We will review each important metric and how it should be interpreted so you can effectively act upon it. The important thing to understand is that you need to act whenever you see an opportunity to improve. However, be careful that you do not act too quickly. A great deal of what you will learn about the success of your business will only be visible over a period of time.

We created the spreadsheet to be a monthly record and not a daily one because there are too many fluctuations that can occur in the short term. The most important way to analyze metrics for websites is to look at trends. Analyzing trends tells you if you are improving, declining, or staying the same over a period of time. Most of your organic tracking is going to trend over months. As we mentioned earlier, your paid advertising trends will be tracked daily, and they should be tracked separately.

Organic Tracking

An important component of organic tracking is the measurement of the traffic to your landing pages. Search engines are crawling your entire site. They are often indexing and listing multiple pages within your site, and they could list any one of them in response to a search or query. In addition, you may be directing visitors to a particular landing page through your networking, advertising, and marketing strategy.

If you have blog pages that become popular, you may have people linking to them or tweeting them, so these pages may temporarily become important landing pages. It's important to understand that when we are tracking our website traffic, we are aware of the pages visitors are landing and, in some cases, from which pages they are exiting.

Total Visits

Visits are the most common and essential piece of data to track organically. In order to track your conversion rate, the first metric you will need to capture is Total Visits. It is important to know the details about the source of your visits. We recommend that you follow these four organic visitor metrics closely.

Search Engines

Knowing the number of visits from search engines is critical because it is telling you how effective your SEO activities are. You can track the number of visits by each search engine easily in StatCounter. You may be surprised at how different the results are among search engines. This may be due to some strength or weakness of your SEO plan. StatCounter has a menu item called *Search Engine Wars,* which displays the traffic from each search engine.

Direct Traffic

Direct traffic refers to those people who entered your domain name in the browser without using a search engine. This metric will tell you several things:

- You have a generic domain name that is highly effective.

- You have repeat customers who know your URL.

- You have established a brand outside of SEO, and people know your domain name from a brochure, billboard, or some other traditional marketing technique.

Direct Traffic will tell you if the hot air balloon you rented with Flowershizzle.com printed on the side was an effective marketing strategy! Additionally, if you are sending out e-mails as part of your marketing strategy, some of those visits may also be captured as direct. If the visitors clicked on a link from their desktop e-mails, the clicks will be categorized as direct. If they clicked on it from a web-based e-mail application like Gmail, you will see that captured in the referral category. One of the ways to ensure you can separately track an email campaign is to point the link in the email to a unique landing page.

Referrals

Referrals will show you if someone clicked on a link to your site from another web site. All analytics providers will show you the exact name and page from where the link came. Referrals are the most significant metric to inform you about the impact of your networking strategy and will show if people come from Facebook, a Blog, Twitter, etc. The link may also come from directories you may have joined, and it may also show if someone clicks on your site from the individual's web email account. If you are aggressively networking, you may want to track each individual source as a separate item under referrals.

Bounce Rate

Bounce Rate is a key measurement of the quality of your landing page. The bounce rate percentage listed in Statcounter or Google Analytics is the percentage of people who only visit one page before exiting your site. A high bounce rate may be acceptable if the landing page is the same page where visitors make a purchase. They might not need to go to another page for your Call to Action.

A high bounce rate is not good if visitors exit your site after only viewing your home page or a product description page. For example, if 1000 people visit your homepage and only 200 people also view an additional page, then you have an 80% bounce rate. A lower bounce rate is better.

Bounce rate is the primary measurement to show if you have a clear consistent marketing strategy. That includes everything from your ad effectiveness, to your landing pages, to your alignment between your networking approach and your website. If you are constantly networking about interesting, yet personal, topics, and you sign your name with your website for your business, visitors may be curious about what you do for a living and click on the link. However, they will most likely exit your site immediately afterwards.

There are several additional metrics regarding visitors that are interesting, however, you do not need to add them to the tracking worksheet at this point. The ones we reviewed will identify the most important actionable information. Both Pam and I have become very effective at living by the 80/20 rule, which emphasizes the approach to focus on the minimum amount of effort that will provide the maximum value.

Actions

You will want to track whatever actions you defined in you conversion approach. It could be a sale, a click on an advertisement, or even the completion of a survey where you capture an e-mail address for your marketing database. These actions are probably not visible from your analytics tool, but they will come from your sales or e-commerce tool. Some tools will help you track actions. Google's Website Optimizer® tool will allow you to put a code snippet on your sales confirmation page, for example, in order to track the conversion. Initially, you will not need sophisticated tools to tell you how many sales you have made; you will probably be watching your sales very closely.

Conversion Rate

As we mentioned previously, understanding and improving the conversion rate will ultimately manage the success of your business. You will calculate the conversion rate as the total number of Call to Actions divided by the number of total number of visits and convert the answer to a percentage. This number is extremely critical to track for your paid advertising strategy as well.

Google PageRank

Google PageRank is the most overanalyzed and overvalued metric that you will come across. SEO companies are making millions selling services that they say can change your Google Page Rank even though Google says it is not an important metric. Here is their perspective listed in the Google Webmaster Forum,

> "Don't worry (about PageRank). In fact, do not bother thinking about it. We only update the PageRank displayed in Google Toolbar a few times a year; this is our respectful hint for you to worry less about PageRank, which is just one of over 200 signals that can affect how your site is crawled, indexed and ranked. PageRank is an easy metric to focus on, but just because it's easy does not mean it's useful for you as a site owner. If you're looking for metrics, we'd encourage you to check out Analytics, think about conversion rates, ROI (return on investment), relevancy, or other metrics that actually correlate to meaningful gains for your website or business. "(Google Webmaster Tools Help)[v]

We could not have said it better. PageRank has become popular because when you download the Google Toolbar for your browser, toolbar.google.com, you can see the PageRank of any site you are visiting just by clicking on a button. Because this is so easy to track, SEO companies have overemphasized this ranking and spend too much time focusing on it. Do not ignore it completely though because if it increases it should indicate that your SEO is trending in the right direction.

Backlinks

As we have discussed, links to your site, called backlinks, are a key part of your SEO strategy. Measuring your effectiveness at creating backlinks is important because it reflects not only the effort you are putting into networking but also the effort you are putting into your overall marketing strategy.

There are several tools to track backlinks. They are listed in the Appendix. All the search engines webmaster tools also track backlinks. You can also track backlinks yourself simply by typing your complete URL into a search engine and seeing how many results you have. The problem with this particular metric is that every tool reports it differently, and we have used a number of them. For example, I recently launched a website, and after the first month of applying my SEO strategy, I had the following results when I checked my backlink total from different sources:

Source	# of Backlinks
Google Toolbar	1
Google Search Results	105
Google Webmaster Tools	6,633
Yahoo Site Explorer	7,996
Bing Toolbox	2,902
3rd Party Tool	4,352

So, as you can see, the variability is considerable. I think the most important result is the number of times you show up in search results. That is a "real time" view of your presence on the internet. For tracking purposes, just select a single tool and enter the results monthly. Do not change tools. Also, do not worry if the number sometimes varies up and down; that is just another quirk of these tools.

Search Engine Results Position (SERP)

SERP is the last and most notable measurement of the effectiveness of your SEO strategy. SERP tracking captures the page number in search engine results that you show up for specific keywords. For example, if you search Google for "Flower Deliver in Plymouth", and you find http://www.plymouthflowerstore.com on page 3 of Google's results, then the SERP position is 3. Obviously, the results depend on what keyword or keyword phrase you use.

The first step to track SERP results is to review the keywords or keyword phrases that you identified in the Optimization Phase. Write in the top three keywords on the Tracking Checklist that you want to follow. You may want to initially track your company name as a keyword as well. The next step is identifying the SERP results for each keyword. One approach to do this could be to type the keywords in a search engine and scroll through pages until you find your website, however, I would not recommend this approach. Instead, have a tool do it for you. Fortunately, this is a free service offered by several sites. (See the Appendix for a listing of sites that offer this service free of charge.) The most important aspect of tracking SERP is to use the same keywords and same search engines each month. Note that the ranking can vary from month to month depending on your SEO strategy and the strategies of your competitors.

○ **Important:** Tracking SERP will also alert you if you have been de-indexed due to a penalty.

Advertising Tracking

Advertising Tracking is fairly simple. It assumes that you are already performing organic tracking. Advertising tracking differs in that you may want to track daily instead of monthly until you refine your ads. Otherwise there is a potential cost associated with allowing poor performing ads to remain. The most important unique tracking components are:

Impressions

Impressions tell you how many times your ad showed up on a page. This gives you the overall opportunity that your ad could be read. It does not mean it was read or even seen, but it reflects its potential.

Clicks

Clicks are the only real metric in advertising. A click on an ad means that you are most likely paying for it, and it means you are bringing a potential customer to your site.

Click Through Rate (CTR)

CTR is an important metric to help you understand the effectiveness of your advertising campaign. CTR is the number of clicks divided by the number of impressions. This is usually a very small number, such as 10 clicks per 1000 impressions, which is a 1% CTR. The CTR will force you to question the effectiveness of your ad. You will have to continually ask yourself the following questions in order to improve your CTR:

- Is my ad properly aligned with my keywords?

- Are my ads posted in the right locations?

- Is the ad text appealing?

This illustrates why you may want to have multiple ads running simultaneously--- so you can test ad text. If your keywords are focused, but your ad is poorly written, you will have a low CTR. My most successful CTR with AdWords has been 4%.

Validate Cost and ROI

At the end of the first month of advertising tracking, you can review your sales revenues and advertising costs to see if a paid advertising approach is cost effective and if you are achieving your anticipated ROI. There are two ways to validate your ROI for your business model: fixed cost or percentage of sales. You may have established a budget based upon a percentage of your sales. If you had an advertising budget of 10% of sales, then you spent $10 dollars on advertising for every $100 in sales. You may be trying to grow your business rapidly, so you have a fixed budget of $100 in advertising to see how much business you can create.

You need to monitor your budget closely so that you do not run out of the investment that you committed to in the Launch phase. To run an internet business--or any business--you need to constantly track revenue and expenses. If you committed to a financial model when you launched your business, follow it closely to ensure you remain in business. Remember, there are other ways to grow other than paying for advertising, so do not get discouraged if you have limited resources to spend each month.

Chapter 9: Maintain

Maintenance Phase Checklist

The following table lists the steps necessary to perform ongoing Maintenance for your website. Note that there is not a "completed by" column in this phase. Use this checklist to track your progress in this phase. The section that follows includes descriptions of each of the steps listed below.

Steps	Target Date
Refresh and Enhance Content	
Maintain Internet Presence	
Manage Website Quality	
Review for Broken Links	
Review for Duplicate Content	
Review HTML	
Review Site for Penalty Criteria	
Recover from bans	

Maintenance Phase Description

The Maintenance Phase does not introduce many new concepts but is, nonetheless, the most important phase. Many people have the enthusiasm to build and launch a website and internet business; far fewer people know (and do) what it takes to maintain and grow that business.

We know that the get-rich-quick stories flood your email and news articles daily, but, as Pam will tell you, a great deal of that is a myth. Pam is a poster child for this myth. People look at her lifestyle, traveling the country in an RV and taking weeks off from work at a time, and they assume she got lucky or stumbled upon a get-rich-quick scheme. The reality is that her success has only been possible after thousands of hours of building her business to the point where many of the maintenance activities have been automated or outsourced. Through trial and error, Pam created a strong business model and maintenance plan, and now enjoys the fruits of her labor.

We all want to get to where Pam is. However, it is only with patience and a meticulous step-by-step approach that the rest of us will achieve the same results. Fortunately, you will not have to make all the same mistakes Pam made, and you will be able to focus more time on successful strategies for growing your business.

Refresh and Enhance Content

Once you are comfortable with your site and SEO plan, you need to practice the content strategies we discussed. In summary, this is done through the following approaches:

- Update your web pages with current and fresh content such as new products, testimonials, reviews, etc.

- Blog on a scheduled basis either internally, externally or both. Only blog if you have interesting and quality content that will retain and attract a following.

Maintain Internet Presence

Be consistent with those strategies which reflect your strengths and have been successful marketing strategies for you:

- Network weekly on whatever platform that you have chosen, whether it be Facebook, Twitter, Commenting or Social Bookmarking.

- Continue to write articles and press releases as your business grows and evolves. Self-promote and submit press releases when you hit certain milestones such as number of visitors, sales, customers, etc.

- Advertise as necessary when you launch new products or services or to test-market different keyword strategies.

Maintain Website Quality

In the first phases and months of launching your internet business, you will accumulate some baggage on your website. Over time, this baggage becomes garbage and you need to get rid of it to improve and maintain your SEO. In the following section, we discuss some of the more common areas within your website content that need to be maintained. Some of these items will be apparent when you run an analysis with one of the SEO tools we listed in the Appendix. Moreover, all of the search engines' webmaster tools have sections which measure quality aspects of your site, and they will tell you what problems are most important to them. (For the remainder of this chapter when we use the term tool, we are referring to either your development tool, SEO Analysis tool, or search engine webmaster tool.)

Fix Broken Links

Your tool will tell you if you have any broken links on your site. Search engines will devalue your site if you have a lot of broken links because it will slow down their effort to crawl your site, and it will tell them that you are not maintaining it properly. Causes of broken links are:

- Typos: You have incorrectly typed the link on your site

- Changed or deleted pages: You renamed or deleted a page and did not modify the link

- External changes: You may have linked to someone else's site or subpage that is no longer there.

The good news is that these are very easy to fix. Simply correct the error, and the next time you run the tool it should have clean results. See the Appendix for a site that will specifically validate all your backlinks.

Review for Duplicate Content

Your tool will tell you if you have duplicate content on your pages. It will notice if you have the same title or description. It may also notice if you are displaying the same information, such as a product listing, with different sorts of criteria and whether it is creating a duplicate content flag. Search engines do not like duplicate content because they do not know which page is more important. There are several ways to resolve this issue:

- Change the Content: You may not have realized that you had identical titles or descriptions, so you just need to update them. That is an easy fix.

- Use 301 Redirects: Unless you tell them otherwise, search engines see *www.plymouthflowerstore.com*, *plymouthflowerstore.com*, *www.plymouthflowerstore.com/index.htm*, or any other version of your homepage as different sites. As you know, if you type any of these into your browser each will all bring you to the same site. The difference is that when people create links to one or the other, search engines and analytics tools will see them as different sites. Depending on your hosting type, the ways to fix the multiple URL issue can differ. Contact your hosting company to see how to employ 301 redirects. See the Appendix for a tool that will validate whether your redirect is operating as expected.

Review HTML

You may not be a software development guru, and your designer may not be one either. There are some simple and user-friendly tools to determine whether your site is developed according to industry standards. You may have purchased a template or hired a designer who gave you a nice look and feel, but you may not realize if the underlying HTML development was properly coded. Poor quality HTML coding may be visible to search engines and even some visitors. For example, since HTML is constantly evolving and being upgraded to be consistent with its use, a website written for version 4 of Internet Explorer® may not look the same on Internet Explorer version 9 or on Firefox® or Safari®. Some of these HTML errors can also impact your ranking with search engines. Here are several easy ways to check if your HTML has errors:

Browser Checker:

There are several tools and sites that you can use to test your site to determine whether or not it looks the same on different browsers. If you go to http://browsershots.org, you will find a free tool that demonstrates how your website looks on over 60 different browsers. I always check my website on different browsers because, as a Mac user, I sometimes come across sites in Safari that do not work. Therefore, I have to go to Firefox and vice versa. For those of you who are PC users, see the following table from Wik-

ipedia for browser usage as of August 2011 to understand that IE
no longer has the majority of the market[vi]:

Browser	Market Share
Internet Explorer	38.9%
Firefox	25.5%
Google Chrome	20.2%
Safari	7.7%
Opera	2.9%
Mobile browsers	7.1%

HTML Checker:

The World Wide Web Consortium (W3C) is a non-profit organization that maintains all of the standards for the HTML. They have
several free tools to evaluate if your site is built properly.
http://validator.w3.org will analyze your HTML and identify any
coding errors. Some of these errors will not mean anything to you
and may not be important; others will be obvious. If you do not
understand, just search on the error, or work with your developer
to clean up your site.

Text Review:

Search engines do not see images or videos when they crawl your
site. They only see the underlying HTML and content text. There
are tools that allow you to see your site as a search engine would. I
began developing websites just using Notepad® to write the
HTML. It was simple and straightforward and it worked. I knew
every line of HTML intimately, so I knew if there was anything
unnecessary or wrong. Now, everyone is either using a template or

a sophisticated tool to develop their website, and they no longer look at the HTML. Unfortunately, that is all search engines can see. I use a free tool http://www.yellowpipe.com/yis/tools/lynx/ lynx view-er.php to view the HTML of my website text. It shows what your site looks like without any colors or images. It also shows what is in the Alt tags for images, if there is hidden text, etc. This is a great tool not only to make sure that your site is optimized, but also to proofread your content without the distraction of images and video.

Review Site for Penalty Criteria

A penalty can occur if a search engine thinks you are trying to trick it into ranking you higher than your competitors. You do this by taking shortcuts or misrepresenting the quality of your site. If you are penalized, you could be dropped down in your search engine results or you could be de-indexed altogether. You will not get an email saying you are penalized. You will, however, notice a significant decrease in your organic traffic. If you follow the steps we have delineated in this guide, then you should not run into penalties. Sometimes, though, through either neglect or just inexperience, you may get yourself in trouble with search engines. Here are some of the common things to avoid:

Hidden Text:

Strategies such as putting white text on a white background, using super small fonts, or negative indenting of text (so it does not show on the screen) were early black hat or unethical approaches for hiding keywords. That is a big no-no, and those strategies will surely get you penalized. By performing the text review listed above, you can determine if you have done it accidentally.

Linking From or To Banned Sites:

Be careful whom you link to or submit links to. Use the Google toolbar to make sure that anyone you link to has a PageRank higher than 1. This is a good use of the Google PageRank, because if the site has been banned by Google, it will show "not listed." A zero rank is not necessarily bad. It just shows that the site is new and has poor SEO. However a "not listed" ranking is a bad sign.

Trading Links:

Do not get into the habit of trading links with other people. I get emails all the time asking, "If you show mine, I'll show yours." Sound unethical? It is. Remember, Google is trying to determine if the content on your site is more valuable than your competition in order to give you a better ranking. It can tell if you are just trading links to increase your SEO. As people invent obvious unethical practices to trick Google, Google will just modify their algorithm. Remember, if it sounds too good to be true, it probably is.

Keyword Stuffing:

This is difficult to quantify. Some of your content may feel very keyword heavy, especially if it is in a very specific blog. Some tools will help you try to identify this, but if you follow the ethical practices laid out in this guide then you will be fine.

In the Appendix, I have included a link to Google's quality guidelines in the event you are looking for more information. Remember, anything that will impact your ranking with Google will most likely impact the other search engines as well. The good news is that approaching your SEO the way we recommend will put you *way ahead of most of your competitors.* Those people who take shortcuts may initially get more traffic, but in the long term, sites that are well built with quality content will have the most success. If you had a brick and mortar business, you would have to keep it painted and you would have to update the furnishings now and then if you wanted to keep your customers; the internet is no different. Building your site and launching it may feel like the hard parts, but in reality, the hardest part is maintaining it and keeping it a quality site so that your visitors keep coming back.

Recover From bans

If you think you have been banned, go to Google and type in *site: <domain name>* such as *site:www.plymouthflowerstore.com*. If your site does not show up, you have most likely been removed from Google's index. If you find yourself banned, I recommend watching the Google video listed in the Appendix. Basically, you have to review your site for the types of penalty criteria listed above, make the changes, and submit your site to Google for reconsideration. The site to submit to is listed in the Appendix. Google seems committed to working with users to get their sites re-indexed.

Chapter 10: Conclusion

I will make this quick since you have a lot of work to do...

Pursue your dream to be a successful and independent entrepreneur. Adopt the SEO Manifesto as your personal manifesto. Know that through a commitment to follow the processes outlined in this guide that you will attract more customers and you will prosper.

Do not get intimidated by this guide if you are just starting out. Look on the bright side. This guide is a tool that will help you build your online business without having to go through all the trial and error that Pam did.

As you may have noticed, this is not a get-rich-quick book. If you were looking for that, you may need to go back to searching. Let me know when you find one that actually works. My personal experience with successful entrepreneurs--and I know a lot of them--is that hard work, tenacity, risk taking, and the ability to learn and adapt have made them successful. They all have one thing in common: they are not afraid to fail, and they see every failure as a learning opportunity. I sincerely hope that this guide will allow you to take advantage of the opportunities created through someone else's trial and error.

Use Pam's story as motivation. Pam has been successful in a very, very competitive space through passion, persistence, and the commitment to learn and grow. She is constantly looking for ways to improve, and she is not afraid to take risks. As we have mentioned, the biggest risk at this point is your time and effort. So go for it, good luck, and let us know how you are doing.

– Dan and Pam

Appendix

Documents

Also see www.SeoManifesto.com/appendix.html for up-to-date documents and resources.

SEO Checklist

Activity	Target Date	Completed Date
1) Getting Started		
Learn The Basics Of SEO		
2) Prepare		
Identify A Product Or Service		
Target An Audience		
Research Market And Competitors		
Define ROI		
Commit!		
3) Launch		
Select Domain Name		
Generic Or Brand Names		
Brainstorming		

Activity	Target Date	Completed Date
Domain Name Availability		
Associated Names		
Domain Name Registration		
Track Costs		
Understand DNS		
Select Hosting Company		
Determine Design Approach		
Determine Hosting Type		
Select Vendor & Track Cost		
Assign DNS To Domain Name		
Storyboarding		
Define All Content Pages		
Define Page Flow And Navigation		
Design Page Layouts		
Create Website		
Develop Home Page		
Upload And Review		
Expand Site		

Activity	Target Date	Completed Date
4) Optimize		
Identify Keywords		
Keyword Research		
Keyword Definition		
Populate Meta Tags		
Title		
Description		
Keywords		
Robots		
Apply Keywords		
Title		
Headings, H1, H2, H3…		
Strong, <Em>, <B>		
Image Attributes		
Anchor Text		
Build Content		
Validate Keyword Use		
Semantic Latent Indexing		

Activity	Target Date	Completed Date
Associate Content With Videos		
Create Unique Content		
Set A Schedule To Maintain		
Optimize Navigation Structure		
# Of Levels		
Breadcrumbs		
Page And Path Names		
Images In Menu		
Absolute URLs		
Create Conversion Strategy		
Construct A Call To Action		
Modify Site		
Ensure Approach Is Trackable		
Review For Poor Design		
5) Submit		
Submit Sites		
Google Webmaster Tools		
Yahoo Site Submission		

Activity	Target Date	Completed Date
Bing Toolbox		
Submit XML Sitemaps		
Create		
Submit To Google		
Submit To Yahoo		
Submit To Bing		
Submit Links		
Link Quality		
Link To Directories		
Link Building Don'ts		
6) Network		
Create Plan And Approach		
Utilize Facebook		
Create Fan Page		
Market Fan Page		
Custom Fan Pages		
Invite Friends To Fan Page		
Advertising On Facebook		

Activity	Target Date	Completed Date
Utilize LinkedIn		
Create Account		
Connect To Colleagues, Classmates		
Post Business Updates		
Advertise		
Utilize Twitter		
Create Account		
Follow People		
Tweet		
Automate		
Utilize YouTube		
Create Account		
Create Content		
Advertise		
Blog, Blog, Blog		
Internal Site		
External Site		
Comment		

Activity	Target Date	Completed Date
Identify Related Blogs And Forums		
Contribute Quality Content		
Use URL In Signature		
Adopt Google +1		
Create G-Mail Profile		
Install 1+ On Your Website		
Network For Likes		
Perform Social Bookmarking		
Digg		
StumbleUpon		
Reddit		
Delicious		
7) Advertise		
Create Plan And Approach		
Create Conversion Approach		
Establish Landing Pages		
Test And Validate		
Organic Online Advertising		

Activity	Target Date	Completed Date
Create And Submit Press Releases		
Create And Submit Articles		
Paid Advertising		
Establish Budget		
Select Providers		
Write Ads		
Post Ads		
8) Track		
Capture Analytics		
Select Provider		
Utilize Monthly SEO Tracking Spread sheet		
Analyze And Act		
Organic Tracking		
Advertising Tracking		
9) Maintain Website		
Refresh And Enhance Content		
Maintain Internet Presence		
Manage Website Quality		

Activity	Target Date	Completed Date
Fix Broken Links		
Review For Duplicate Content		
Review Html		
Review Site For Penalty Criteria		
Recover From Bans		

Monthly Tracking Checklist

Organic Tracking	Month 1	Month 2	Month...
Total Visits			
Search Engines			
Direct			
Referrals			
Source 1			
Source 2			
Source 3			
Bounce Rate			
Actions			
Conversion Rate			
Google PageRank			
Backlinks			
Search Engine Results Position (SERP)			
Keyword 1			
Keyword 2			
Keyword 3			
Advertising Tracking	**Day 1**	**Day 2**	**Day...**
Impressions			
Clicks			
Click Through Rate			

Resources

The following websites, companies, and resources listed provide the products or services referred to in *The SEO Manifesto*. We are not providing this list as a review or testimonial to their services. As a good consumer, you should research and compare these services based upon your individual needs.

Domain Name Providers (also for checking domain name availability)

http://www.networksolutions.com

http://www.dotster.com

Website Development:

Freelance Individuals:

http://www.elance.com

http://www.odesk.com

http://click2work.com

Companies:

http://www.hotdoodle.com

http://www.jigsy.com

http://www.1800homepage.com

Templates

http://www.dreamtemplate.com

http://landingpagetemplates.us

http://www.easystartertemplates.com

Hosting Companies

http://www.1and1.com

http://www.aplus.net

http://www.hostgator.com

http://www.GoDaddy.com

http://www.yola.com

http://www.fastdomain.com

http://bluehost.com

Keyword Tools

Free

http://adwords.google.com/select/KeywordToolExternal

https://freekeywords.wordtracker.com/

Paid

http://www.spyfu.com/

http://www.sitemapdoc.com/Keyword-Analyzer.aspx

http://productnamekeywords.com/

http://www.keywordresearchpro.com/

SEO Analysis Tools

Free

http://www.seoworkers.com/tools/analyzer.html

http://www.webtoolsnow.com

http://www.pearanalytics.com

Paid

http://www.seoelite.com

http://www.visitors2you.com

http://www.prodevseo.com

Search Engine Submission

Google Webmaster Tools

http://www.google.com/webmasters/

Yahoo Site Submission

http://siteexplorer.search.yahoo.com

Bing Toolbox

http://www.bing.com/toolbox/home/

Online Advertising Management

http://www.marinsoftware.com/pro

http://www.miva.com

Sitemap Creators (Free)

http://www.sitemapsubmit.net/generate-sitemap/

http://www.sitemapdoc.com

http://www.xml-sitemaps.com

Twitter Followers

http://www.socialoomph.com

http://friendorfollow.com

http://huitter.com/mutuality/

http://dossy.org/twitter/karma/

http://www.flashtweet.com

http://www.buzzom.com

http://tweetadder.com

Social Bookmarking

http://www.digg.com

http://www.stumbleupon.com

http://www.reddit.com

http://www.delicious.com

Press Releases

http://www.24-7pressrelease.com

http://www.prweb.com

http://prlog.com

Article Sites

http://www.squidoo.com

http://www.hubpages.com

http://www.gather.com

http://www.advogato.org

SERP Tracking

http://www.sitemapdoc.com/Serp-Rank.aspx

http://www.serptracker.org

Affiliate Brokers

http://www.cj.com

http://www.clickbank.com

https://www.linkbank.com

Graphic Designers for Ads

Freelance Designers:

http://www.elance.com

http://www.odesk.com

http://click2work.com

Backlinks Counters

https://www.google.com/webmasters/tools/

https://siteexplorer.search.yahoo.com

http://www.bing.com/toolbox/home/

http://www.linkvendor.com/seo-tools/domain-popularity.html

Maintain Website Quality

Validate Broken Links:

http://validator.w3.org/checklink

Validate 301 Redirects:

http://www.webconfs.com/redirect-check.php

Browser Viewer:

http://browsershots.org

Validate HTML:

http://validator.w3.org

Text Review:

http://www.yellowpipe.com/yis/tools/lynx/lynx_viewer.php

Quality Guidelines:

http://www.google.com/support/webmasters/bin/answer.py?answer=35769&topic=8522#3

Recover from bans:

http://googlewebmastercentral.blogspot.com/2009/04/tips-on-requesting-reconsideration.html

Requests for Reconsideration from Google:

https://www.google.com/webmasters/tools/reconsideration?pli=1

Glossary

301	Status Code: tells search engines if you have moved or deleted a web page
404	Status Code: Not Found – the result you see if you go to a web page that no longer exists
Abandonment Rate	The rate at which begin the process of performing your Call to Action but never complete it.
Affiliate	Someone who has a license agreement to market another company's goods or services usually for a commission based upon a sale, a click or a lead
B2B	Business to Business
B2C	Business to Consumer
BODY	The portion of an HTML document that contains the document's content
Bounce Rate	The percentage of people who exit the site after only viewing one page
Call to Action	A response that you want to get from a visitor on your site including a purchase, survey or download.
CPC	Cost Per Click: the typical way online advertisers charge. You pay only if someone clicks on your ad
CPM	CPM or Cost per thousand (the M represent the roman numeral for 1000)

Crawl	A slang term used to define how search engines find your site and all of its associated pages
CTR	Click Through Rate: the percentage of people who click on your website link out of the total number who see it
DMOZ	Directory Mozilla: the largest free online directory of websites
DNS	Domain Name System
FAQ	Frequently Asked Question
FTP	File Transfer Protocol
H1, H2, H3, H4, H5, H6	Heading Levels 1, 2, 3, 4, 5, 6: A heading format element in HTML
HEAD	The HEAD element is the portion of HTML document that contains hidden information about a web page, such as its title and keywords
HTML	Hypertext Markup Language: the primary language in which web pages are written
Impressions	The number of times a webpage or advertisement is shown to a visitor
Index	Where search engines collect and store information about a website
ISP	Internet Service Provider

META	Metadata: the hidden information in the HEAD of HTML that defines certain aspects about your website for search engines <meta http-equiv="content-type" content=""> <meta name="robots" content=""> <meta name="description" content=""> <meta name="keywords" content=""> <meta name="author" content="">
SEM	Search Engine Marketing
SEO	Search Engine Optimization
SERPs	Search Engine Results Pages
TITLE	Document Title: in the HEAD of HTML where authors should identify the contents of a web page
Troll	A person who comments on public forums to either sabotage the blog or promote unrelated products or services
URL	Uniform Resource Locator: http://www.example.com
W3C	World Wide Web Consortium
XML	Extensible Markup Language (file.xml)

References

i *comScore Releases April 2011 U.S. Search Engine Rankings.* (2011, May 11). Retrieved November 1, 2011, from comScore.com: http://www.comscore.com/Press_Events/Press_Releases/2011/5/comScor e_Releases_April_2011_U.S._Search_Engine_Rankings

ii *U.S Small Business Administration Frequently Asked Questions.* (n.d.). Retrieved November 1, 2011, from SBA.gov: http://web.sba.gov/faqs/faqIndexAll.cfm?areaid=24

iii *Google Webmaster Tools Help.* (n.d.). Retrieved November 1, 2011, from Google.com: http://www.google.com/support/webmasters/bin/answer.py?answer=473

iv *Youtube.com Traffic and Demographic Statistics by Quantcast.* (n.d.). Retrieved November 1, 2011, from quantcast.com: http://www.quantcast.com/youtube.com

v *Google FAQ: Crawling, indexing & ranking .* (n.d.). Retrieved November 1, 2011, from Google.com: http://sites.google.com/site/webmasterhelpforum/en/faq--crawling-- indexing---ranking

vi *Wikipedia Usage share of web browsers according to StatCounter.* (n.d.). Retrieved November 1, 2011, from Wikipedia.com: http://en.wikipedia.org/wiki/Usage_share_of_web_browsers

www.ingramcontent.com/pod-product-compliance
Lightning Source LLC
Chambersburg PA
CBHW071158050326
40689CB00011B/2171